Themes for Listening and Speaking

Self-study/Teacher's edition

Carole Robinson and Helen Parker

Oxford University Press

Oxford University Press
Walton Street, Oxford OX2 6DP

Oxford New York Toronto Delhi Bombay
Calcutta Madras Karachi Petaling Jaya
Singapore Hong Kong Tokyo Nairobi Dar es Salaam
Cape Town Melbourne Auckland

and associated companies in
Beirut Berlin Ibadan Nicosia

OXFORD is a trade mark of Oxford University Press

ISBN 0 19 432793 0

First published 1986
Second impression 1987

Illustrations by:
David Ace
Jill Downie
Simon Gooch
Joanna Quinn

Printed in Hong Kong

Acknowledgements
The publishers would like to thank the following for permission to reproduce photographs:

Camera Press
Michael Cole Camerawork
Richard and Sally Greenhill
Christopher Moore
Jill Posener
Rex Features

Photographs by:
Nicky Dixon
Rob Judges
Julian Prentis

In addition, the authors would like to thank their advanced students at Oxford College of Further Education.

Contents

Introduction

Aim

Themes for Listening and Speaking has been designed for all advanced students of English who need to improve their listening and speaking skills. The authentic recordings are thought-provoking, challenging, instructive and fun. The material will interest and motivate students preparing for Papers 4 and 5 of the Cambridge Certificate of Proficiency in English examination, and the RSA advanced Communicative Use of EFL exam (CUEFL), and non-exam students alike.

How to approach the book

The book has been organized to give maximum flexibility. By consulting the Lesson Planner at the front of the book, it is possible to follow a variety of paths through the units. Each of the columns in the grid may be taken as a starting point, so a unit could be selected on the basis of the topic, or on linguistic criteria. For example, if you wanted to explore the theme of women in society, you could organize a series of lessons around Units 4, 8, 19 and 21, and so on with other themes. Alternatively, if more practice in coping with non-British English accents is needed, then you could choose selections from Units 1, 2, 3, 5, 8, 9, 11, 18 and 23. For students who need to heighten their awareness of the importance of stress and intonation in conveying a message, Units 4, 13, 15 and 18 would be useful.

The Unit

Each unit is divided into three sections. The Listening section contains a task or tasks based on an authentic recording. A Practice section follows, in which students are given exercises on function, structure, vocabulary, stress and intonation related to the listening material. Finally, there is a Speaking section which provides a variety of communicative activities based around the theme of the unit.

Notes for the teacher

The material is suitable for use either in a class with a teacher and a cassette player, in a monitored language laboratory, or by an individual student in a listening centre or at home. The teacher, after listening to the recording, must decide on a teaching strategy which is appropriate for both the material and the students. The following notes offer some suggestions for using *Themes for Listening and Speaking*.

Listening

• Is a 'warm-up' to the topic necessary?

It is often inappropriate just to switch on the cassette player and ask students to listen. In real life we usually have some idea of what we are going to listen to, and are mentally prepared for the topic or situation. Occasionally, though, a 'warm-up' may destroy the element of surprise, e.g. Unit 18 Help!

• What forms could a warm-up take?

–students try to predict the content of the unit from the title, e.g. Unit 3 While you were out, and then listen to check their predictions.
–students pool what knowledge they have on a subject, e.g. Unit 23 A Hollywood story.
–a very short section of the recording is played, for students to guess at the likely setting and/or topic, e.g. Unit 17 Jobspot.
–an object, photograph or illustration from a book is shown to the students to stimulate a brief discussion, e.g. Unit 14 After a fashion.

• Does any of the vocabulary need to be pre-taught?

Much of the meaning can be inferred from the context. This is a vital skill to develop in students, so it is important not to pre-teach too much of the vocabulary in a recording. However, in some of the more demanding recordings, students would not be able to complete the task without the pre-teaching of key words, e.g. Unit 7 Plain sailing. It is also crucial that students understand the task, and this may involve checking and/or pre-teaching the vocabulary.

• Should the recording be played through from beginning to end without stopping?

This depends on many factors: length and difficulty of both recording and task, unfamiliar accent, and the experience of the students. More pausing and repetition will be needed in the early stages of a course. It is often advisable to listen for gist prior to listening intensively to complete a specific task, e.g. Unit 19 Coping.

• What is listening for gist?

Listening to understand the general idea, while not being distracted by the details, or confused by hesitations, redundancies and backtracking. Listening for gist is a very important skill to develop in students, who can easily be discouraged by authentic material if they think they have to understand every word. In order to develop this skill, there are some apparently 'difficult' recordings which have a relatively simple task, e.g. Unit 12 Eccentrics and Unit 22 What's on?

• What about checking the answers?

Before the answer is given, students can confer with a classmate and compare their answers once the task has been completed. If there is a difference of opinion, replay the tape, stopping and checking at the relevant section.
For some tasks, answers are most easily given using the board, a copy of the completed exercise, or an over-head projector transparency, e.g. Unit 7 Plain sailing and Unit 20 And later today.

Practice

This section is designed as a bridge between the receptive listening activities and the freer, productive Speaking section. There is a change of emphasis from *what* is said for the completion of the listening task, to *how* it is said.

• Do we work straight through the practice section?

This depends. The Practice section may be used either to round off work on the Listening section, or as preparation for the Speaking.

Speaking

In the Speaking section, the intention is that students should become engrossed in *what* is said rather than *how* it is said: the linguistic expertise and accuracy should have been gained in the Practice section. This section is therefore for developing fluency.

• What is the role of the teacher?

–to set up the activity so that the students can work on their own without interference.
–to monitor the activity unobtrusively so that problems can be noted for future reference.
–to intervene in the activity only if it is clearly not working.

• What steps can the teacher take to ensure a successful outcome?

–sufficient preparation by the students is essential for certain of the Speaking tasks. Some of the more serious role plays need careful work, probably at home, e.g. Unit 9 Another country. In other more light-hearted activities, e.g. Unit 6 What's my line? completion of the Practice section should be sufficient.
–the teacher needs to have decided questions of classroom management like layout of the room, size of groups, combinations of students in groups and approximate length of time an activity will take.
–instructions on the activity need to be clear and concise, and students' understanding of what is required must be checked.

• How will the course help students to pass Papers 4 and 5 of the Proficiency exam?

It will expose them to, and involve them in, a wide range of varied authentic material, with diverse accents and tasks. Above all, it should arouse their interest and hence their motivation to learn and succeed in English.

Notes for self-study students

It will be useful to read the Notes for the teacher above, but bear in mind that a different approach is needed.

• What should I do before listening?

Read the task carefully, and check any vocabulary that is unfamiliar. Make sure you understand what you need to listen for in order to complete the task.

• Should I listen straight through the recording without stopping?

Yes, but you may need to train yourself to do this. When you first start using the book, or when you find a unit particularly demanding, play a section at a time, and replay it.

• How do I use the language notes and the tapescript?

If you cannot complete the task, read the language notes, and try again. If you are still stuck, read through the tapescript as a reading exercise and look up in the language items list any vocabulary you feel is crucial to understanding. Then listen again. If you are still having problems, follow the tapescript as you listen. Then try to complete the task.

• How do I use the Answer key?

To check your answers when you feel you have done as much as you can. If your answer is wrong, look at the relevant part of the tapescript, and/or listen again.

• Can I use the Practice section?

Yes. Follow the instructions, and check your answers in the Answer key.

• How can I use the Speaking section?

Some tasks, such as reading aloud and giving instructions, can be done even if you are working alone. In this case, it would be useful to record yourself and listen critically to what you have done. Other tasks clearly demand a partner. Perhaps you could find someone else who is also studying on his/her own.

• Can I use this material for Proficiency exam practice?

Yes. The recordings and exercise types will prepare you for the kind of activities you will be tested on in the exam. Remember that in Paper 4 each recording will be played through twice. Good luck!

Lesson Planner

Unit	Mode/Topic	Speakers
1 Ladies and gentlemen	public announcement: at an international conference	American
2 An Aussie at Eton	interview: an Australian at Britain's most traditional school	RP*; Australian
3 While you were out	telephone: ansaphone messages	RP; American; London; advanced RP
4 A woman's place	conversation: a couple discuss suitable presents for men or women	RP; RP
5 Hard sell	radio: advertisements	American; American
6 What's my line?	radio game: people talk about their work	Irish; RP; Scottish; Northern; RP; Northern
7 Plain sailing	instructions: a teacher explains a sailing course	West Country
8 Till death us do part	conversation: three women discuss marriage in their cultures	Indian; Danish; Brazilian
9 Another country	interview: an immigrant talks about living and working in the UK	RP; Caribbean
10 Local government	lecture: a lecturer explains government and education	RP
11 Spot the sport	various: people talk about sports	Australian; RP; London; Canadian; RP
12 Eccentrics	conversation: two friends talk about unusual people	RP; RP
13 Dr Norton's surgery	telephone: a secretary makes an appointment	Midlands; RP
14 After a fashion	talks: two costume museum guides explain some exhibits	RP; RP
15 At a loss for words	conversation: discussion about the influence of one language on another	French; RP
16 Waiting in the wings	radio interview: an aging actress talks on a satirical radio show	RP; RP
17 Jobspot	local radio programme: details of job vacancies	RP; West Country
18 Help!	telephone conversation: a friend asks a favour	American (southern)
19 Coping	conversation: a mother talks about her mentally handicapped son	RP; RP
20 And later today	radio: a preview of the morning's programmes	RP
21 Fairground Dream	song: a girl falls in love at first sight	RP
22 What's on?	conversation: two young people plan a day at an arts festival	RP; RP
23 A Hollywood story	narrative: an actor tells an anecdote	American

*RP = received pronunciation

Listening	Practice	Speaking
note-taking	function: giving instructions	giving instructions
accuracy checking	vocabulary: collocation	discussing the press
taking messages	function: making suggestions; structure: reported speech	role play: a phone conversation
multiple choice comprehension	intonation	discussing an advertisement
multiple choice comprehension; cloze	style; stress	reading aloud
identification	function: withholding information	discussing job qualities and job satisfaction
drawing course on map	vocabulary: definitions	giving and following instructions on a map
note-taking	structure: phrasal and prepositional verbs	discussing marriage customs
matching; true/false comprehension	structure: question forms	role play: a newspaper interview
completing a chart	function: giving examples; asking questions	discussing education
identification	structure: tenses	role play: a spectator at Wimbledon
matching	function: talking about the past	describing a person; limericks
completing a message	style and register	role play: a secretary asks for time off
matching	labelling; vocabulary: suffixes	describing photos; discussing clothes
completing a grid; multiple choice comprehension	function: confirmation; vocabulary: word building	discussing language
multiple choice comprehension	function: interviewing	role play: a chat show
completing a grid	vocabulary: word fields	creating a 'jobspot'
multiple choice comprehension	function: expressing reservation	role play: favours
multiple choice; true/false comprehension	function: signalling interest	discussing problems faced by disabled people
proof-reading	vocabulary: collocation; word building	reading aloud
cloze	pronunciation	discussing pop music
checking	function: making suggestions; agreement/disagreement	role play: planning a social schedule
re-ordering; true/false comprehension	function: story-telling techniques	writing and telling a story

1 Ladies and gentlemen

Listening

A Below are Professor Hunt Williams's notes for the announcements he has to make at the final plenary session of an international conference on urban planning. Listen to his announcements and fill in the missing information.

B Dr Paul van der Sweep is a delegate at the conference, and has been attending the sessions on computer-aided building design. This morning he took notes of the discussion he attended. He is leaving the conference today and is booked on the 17.15 plane. He has always wanted to visit Hawaii. Tick (√) in the box provided, those of Professor Williams's announcements that are relevant to Dr van der Sweep.

1. Final discussion of urban .... will move to Room .... ☐
2. Domestic .... session will move to room .... ☐
3. Return ...... to .... Lodge. ☐
4. Return discussion .... to .... by .... ☐
5. First .... for airport outside .... Building at .... ☐
6. Second .... at .... Delegates to arrive .... ☐
7. Drs Schapsinger, Garbeldi and Surinander: Collect .... from conference .... ☐
8. Dr Goldman (.......... Institute) .....th Annual Convention of ...., in ...., in......... . Interested parties leave .... at conference .... ☐

Practice

A Professor Williams is speaking in a formal, international setting, and his aim is to be very polite and clear. Listen again to the recording, and note down the words the speaker uses to do the following:

1 stop the delegates talking

... I ... have your ... for a moment, please.

2 make polite requests

(discussion records) I ... to ... you return them to the session chairpeople.
(coaches) I'd ... to ... you all to be there, ready for the buses, at least five minutes before the departure times.

3 repeat information

We're moving the final discussion to Room 201. . . . Room 201. Which means that the domestic shelter session will be changed from Room 201 to Room 304. . . . the domestic shelter session in Room 304.

4 finish relaying each piece of information

5 address his audience at the start and finish

B The speaker has to make six announcements. Listen again to the recording and find the words he uses to introduce each new piece of information.

1 (room change) Now, . . ., I'd like to mention
2 (return keys) . . ., I have a . . .
3 . . . to your discussion records
4 . . . coaches for the airport
5 I have . . . for Dr Schapsinger
6 (P.E.S. Convention) . . ., I have a reminder

Speaking

You are a tourist guide. Your coachload of tourists has arrived at its destination, and you have the information below to give them. Using some of the language practised earlier, decide where polite requests would be appropriate and how you would progress from one point to another. Make the speech.

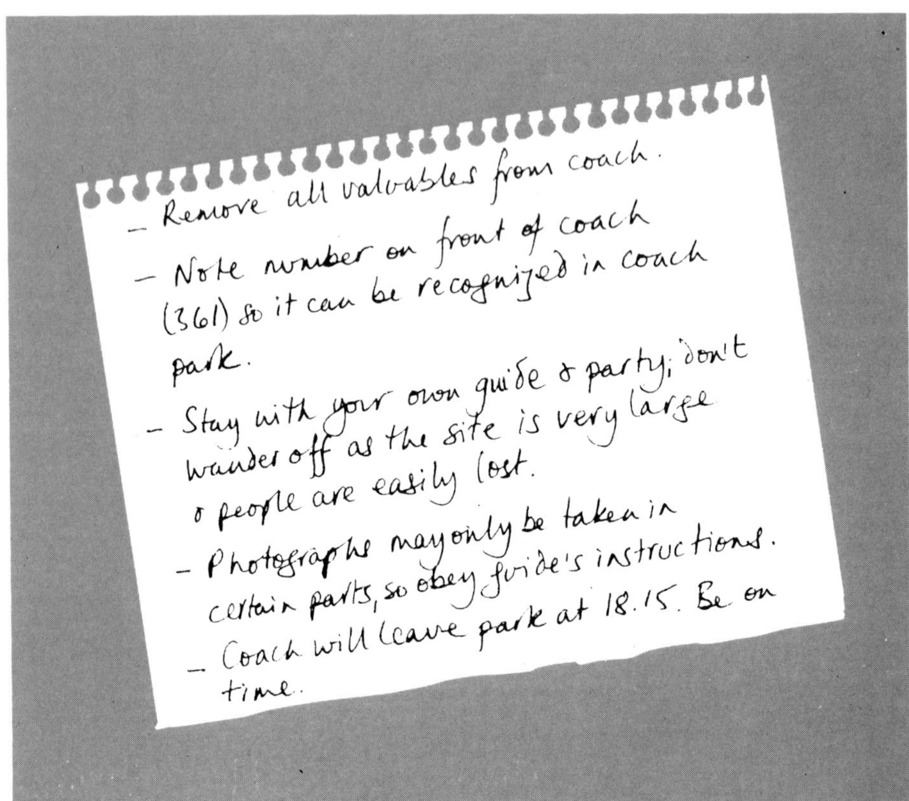

2 An Aussie at Eton

Listening

ETON SHOCK REVELATIONS

Bronzed New Zealander Charles Marston rocked the boat at Eton College last week when he struck out at the £6,000-a-year private school. Charles, thirty, in a frank interview with hard-hitting radio personality, Milly Jarvis, slammed Eton and its traditions. And Charles is not the spoiled brat of an aristocrat, but a teacher at the exclusive public school. Headmaster Dr Raymond Birchett is said to be 'displeased' by Charles's disclosures.

CLOTHES TO GO

Charles revealed that the conspicuous uniform, familiar to residents of Eton village, and worn by both staff and pupils was about to be replaced with 'something more normal' and he also talked openly about the exclusive Eton wall game and field game.

RUDE GESTURES

But the facts which are most likely to worry the £30,000 a year Head are Charles's frank revelations of the breakdown of discipline at Eton. Charles divulged that fights where the younger boys were mobbed by the older ones were a common feature of Eton life. And he admitted that boys frequently make rude gestures at masters. With these blatant examples of anarchy in the 400-year-old school, Charles Marston advised Milly Jarvis not to send her son there.

COLLAPSE?

These exposures came hot on the heels of the scandals recently revealed at Dartington Hall, another of Britain's high-charging private schools. Is this evidence that these last bastions of education and class privilege are fast crumbling? Charles Marston yesterday told our reporter, 'I have no comment to make.'

A A teacher at a famous English school gave an interview about life there. The article above, based on the interview, was submitted to a local newspaper by a student journalist. The editor, however, suspected that certain facts might not be right. He ringed all the points about which he was suspicious. Read the article where you will see these ten facts numbered, and then listen to the recording. On the grid below, mark (T) for true, (F) for false and (N) for no information.

1		2		3		4		5	
6		7		8		9		10	

B Listen again and tick (✓) the correct answers in the boxes provided.

1 When the teacher says he wears 'perfectly normal clothes', he means the clothes he wears are

a ☐ ordinary.
b ☐ in very good condition.
c ☐ odd.
d ☐ comfortable.

2 When the teacher says that Eton offers games that cannot be played in any other part of the world, he

a ☐ is using the programme for publicity.
b ☐ has forgotten what he was going to say.
c ☐ is being ironical.
d ☐ is advertising Eton's positive features.

3 When the interviewer says, 'So you wouldn't recommend that I put my son down for Eton', she is

a ☐ asking for advice on Eton.
b ☐ stating the teacher's views.
c ☐ enquiring for further information on Eton.
d ☐ asking for his opinion on Eton.

Practice

A Look at the list of adjectives below that occur in the recording. Each of the nouns in the circle is paired in the recording with one of these adjectives. Listen again and link each noun with its adjective, then look up in your dictionary any words you still do not understand.

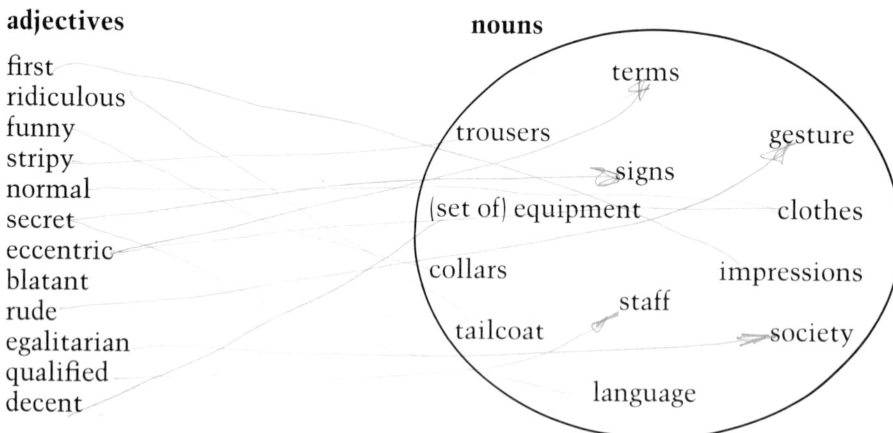

B Use the list of adjectives and nouns to form different pairs, for example, *first language, first signs*. You will notice that many of the adjectives have more than one meaning. Use your dictionary if necessary and try to find at least two nouns to go with each adjective.

Speaking

In small groups, discuss one of the following issues and report back your conclusions to the rest of the class.

Group 1 Newspapers invent news.
Group 2 A 'free press' can never exist as long as we have politicians.
Group 3 Newspapers are unnecessary.
Group 4 Censorship is essential for the sake of national security.
Group 5 Newspapers have a right to distort the truth for entertainment purposes.

3 While you were out

Listening

A Listen to the four recorded messages on Patrick Lechlade's Ansaphone. Put a tick (√) in the box provided beside the name of each caller.

1 ☐ Christopher Orton
2 ☐ Brian Tidmarsh
3 ☐ Sam Schoenberg
4 ☐ Jenny Pargeter
5 ☐ Wayne Jones
6 ☐ Antonia North
7 ☐ Marty Hunt
8 ☐ Joan Orton

B The keypoints of the Ansaphone messages were noted down. Listen again, tick (√) the appropriate squares, and complete the notes below. The first message has been done for you.

1

To *Patrick Lechlade* Date *6th March*

WHILE YOU WERE OUT

M*s* *Antonia North* of *'Tatler'*

Phone No —

Telephoned	√	Please ring	√
Called to see you		Will ring again	
Wants to see you	√	Urgent	

Message *Jenny Pargeter wants photo feature on VIP. Suggests lunch Brown's early next week*

Operator *Jon*

2

To .... Date *6th March*

WHILE YOU WERE OUT

M .... of ....

Phone No ....

Telephoned		Please ring	
Called to see you		Will ring again	
Wants to see you		Urgent	

Message *In* .... *few days*
Staying with ....

Operator ....

3

To .... Date *6/3*

WHILE YOU WERE OUT

M .... of ....

Phone No ....

Telephoned		Please ring	
Called to see you		Will ring again	
Wants to see you		Urgent	

Message .... *not available.* .... *or change order?*

Operator ....

4

To .... Date *6 March*

WHILE YOU WERE OUT

M*r* *Marty Hunt* of ....

Phone No ....

Telephoned		Please ring	
Called to see you		Will ring again	
Wants to see you		Urgent	

Message *Wants to* ....

Operator ....

Practice

A Listen to the first three recorded messages again, and note the way in which each of the speakers introduces himself or herself.

1 . . . Antonia North.
2 . . . Sam Schoenberg.
3 . . . Wayne Jones.

B Read the note that Jenny Pargeter left for her secretary, Antonia North. Below are some of the words Antonia North uses to pass on Jenny Pargeter's message politely. Find the words to complete the secretary's sentences.

1 She's . . . me . . . you –
2 . . . see . . . you can do a photographic feature on a VIP.
3 Mrs Pargeter . . . like . . . you at the beginning of next week . . . she's going away.
4 She suggested . . . you . . . to have lunch at Brown's.

Antonia
1. Please ring P. Lechlade.
2. Can he do that photo feature on you-know-who?
3. I'd like to see him early next week as (remember!) I'm off to Vienna on Wed.
4. We can have lunch at Brown's.
Thanks,
V.

Speaking

Student A
You are Jonathan Bell, Patrick Lechlade's personal assistant. Patrick Lechlade has left you this note. Using the language practised above, ring Antonia North. Give the message politely, and arrange a day, time and place for the meeting.

Jon
Ring Jenny P's secretary at 'Tatler'.
Can do feature if it's this month.
Free Mon. or Tues. for lunch, but Tues. better, after 1.00 p.m. Not Brown's – so crowded. Suggest Langham's.
P.

Student B
You are Antonia North, Jenny Pargeter's secretary. Jenny Pargeter has left you this note. Deal with the call from Patrick Lechlade's personal assistant, and negotiate a day, time and place for the meeting.

Antonia
1. Forgot to say – if Patrick L. rings, suggest Mon. 12.30 at Brown's. Tues. poss. but not Wed.
V.

4 A woman's place

Listening

This is a conversation between a husband and wife that takes place one Sunday morning. Read through the questions, then listen to the recording. Tick (√) the appropriate letter, a, b, or c, in the box provided.

1 At the beginning of the conversation Harry is
- **a** ☐ trying to sleep.
- **b** ☐ watching TV.
- **c** ☑ reading the newspaper.

2 At first Harry is
- **a** ☐ very interested.
- **b** ☐ quite interested.
- **c** ☑ only half-listening.

3 What does Anne feel about the advertisement?
- **a** ☒ amused
- **b** ☑ indignant
- **c** ☐ furious

4 According to Anne, the Superchef will
- **a** ☑ keep her in the kitchen.
- **b** ☐ save time and energy.
- **c** ☐ make Christmas happy.

5 The advertisement is trying to persuade
- **a** ☑ men to buy their wives Superchefs.
- **b** ☐ women to persuade husbands to buy them Superchefs.
- **c** ☐ women to buy themselves Superchefs.

6 According to Anne, an equivalent present for a man might be
- **a** ☐ socks.
- **b** ☐ a diamond tie pin.
- **c** ☑ a power tool.

7 What do you think Harry's attitude is to the Women's Liberation Movement?
- **a** ☐ indifferent
- **b** ☐ supportive
- **c** ☑ scornful

8 When Harry says, 'I don't see why she shouldn't be', he means she
- **a** ☐ shouldn't be in the kitchen.
- **b** ☑ should be in the kitchen.
- **c** ☐ should be having a happy Christmas.

9 Anne says, 'It's no use talking to you' because
- **a** ☐ Harry's not listening.
- **b** ☑ Harry's not going to change his attitude.
- **c** ☐ she knows he's not going to buy her a Superchef.

10 By the end of the conversation, has Anne persuaded Harry to appreciate her attitude to the advertisement?

a ☐ yes
b ☑ no
c ☐ probably not

Practice A

1 When Harry says 'Hmm', his voice shows us that he is only mildly interested in what Anne is saying. Listen to the recording again and tick (✓) the alternative which shows this intonation.

a ☐ ⟶
b ☑ ⟶↗
c ☐ ⤴

2 When Anne says, 'Of course it would be useful, dear', she is pointing out to Harry that he hasn't understood. Which word does she stress?

a ☐ Of *course* it would be useful
b ☐ Of course it *would* be useful
c ☑ Of course it would be *useful*

3 When Harry says 'Yes, well, what about her?' he

a ☐ wants to know more.
b ☑ wants Anne to shut up.
c ☐ is surprised.

4 When Harry says, 'Well, you always give me socks, don't you?' because he is not asking a question, his voice goes

a ☑ don't you? ↘
b ☐ don't you? ↗
c ☐ don't you? ↘↗

5 When Harry says, 'plaid socks, plain socks, green socks', are these the only socks she's given him? How do you know?

6 When Anne says, 'Harry, Harry . . .' with a wide pitch range, which of these could she say instead, with the same meaning?

a ☑ You do go on.
b ☐ Oh, you're so sweet.
c ☐ Do shut up.

B In the conversation, Anne and Harry express many moods. Using the categories below, put the appropriate letters in the boxes provided. Some moods are expressed more than once. Check in your dictionary any words that are unfamiliar.

a sarcasm **b** humour **c** irritation **d** resignation **e** ridicule

1 ☐ **Harry** Yes, well, what about her?
2 ☐ **Harry** Are you trying to tell me something, darling?
3 ☐ **Anne** No, of course I don't.
4 ☐ **Harry** Well, you always give me socks, don't you? I've a drawer full of socks: plaid socks, plain socks, green socks . . .
5 ☐ **Harry** She's going to switch this on and it's going to do all these wonderful things . . .
6 ☐ **Anne** With this marvellous kitchen aid . . .
7 ☐ **Harry** Well, I don't see why she shouldn't be.
8 ☐ **Anne** Oh, there's no use talking to you.

Speaking

Look at the picture above and discuss the attitudes and assumptions that lie behind it. Consider the following points.

Is the original advertisement intended to appeal to men, or women, or both equally?
What response to the advertisement is indicated by the graffiti?
What is your own response?
Can you think of any other advertisements that work in the same way?

5 Hard sell

Listening

A Listen to this recording from an American commercial radio station. Then answer the questions below. Where appropriate, tick (√) the letters a, b, or c, in the box provided.

1 What are the brand names of the goods advertised?

2 The first item advertised is probably
- a ☐ a milk drink.
- b ☑ for washing dishes.
- c ☐ soap.

3 The last item advertised is probably
- a ☐ an air freshener.
- b ☑ a fabric conditioner.
- c ☐ a shampoo.

4 The woman's voice is best described as
- a ☑ intimate.
- b ☐ sexy.
- c ☐ persuasive.

5 The advertisement's message is that the goods at the store are
- a ☐ good value for money.
- b ☐ priceless and high quality.
- c ☑ inexpensive but good.

B The leaflet opposite is for the Hepburn Theater's coming season. Listen to the recording again, and fill in the missing information.

Practice

A Listen to the Makeway advertisement again and find six words that are used more than once.

B Listen again to the woman's voice, and find those words that are stressed because the speaker wants listeners to take notice of them.

C Choose brand-names for the following products. Then compose slogans to advertise each one. Try to use the word *even* as it occurs in the recording.

floor polish   toothpaste   low calorie soft drink   air freshener spray

Speaking

Read the passage below silently and then discuss with your partner what it is and where you would see/hear it. Underline the stressed words and then read it aloud for your partner to check.

Colin's crazy clearance sale starts on Friday, 27th July. There are massive price reductions on furniture, carpets and curtain fabrics. You'd have to be out of your mind to miss it. Colin's crazy clearance sale, starting Friday, 27th July, at Colin's, in the Brunel Plaza, Swindon.

HEPBURN THEATER

North 47th St. Seattle

These are just some of the exciting events planned for the .... season.

The __________ Choir
The _____ Bananas
_______ and the Melbas
Opera _______

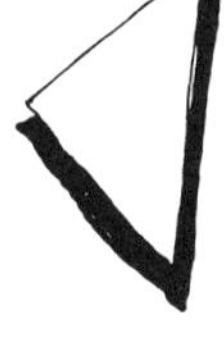

Entertainment for ....

Booking starts ....

Ring the Hepburn Box Office NOW on 9914 4213

For details and dates, see over.

6 What's my line?

Listening

What's my line? was the title of a popular BBC television programme. The aim was to guess the occupation of a person as he/she mimed his/her job. Play a similar game yourself by listening to six people talking about their work. Try to guess the occupation of each and select your answers from the list below. Write the appropriate letters in the boxes provided.

a police officer
b builder
c vet
d actor
e doctor
f traffic warden
g dentist
h photographer
i ambulance-driver
j fire-fighter
k artist
l cook
m welder
n plumber

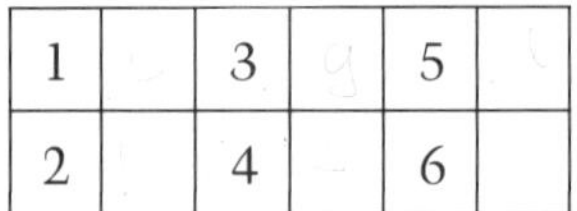

1		3		5	
2		4		6	

Practice

A Read the transcript below and notice how the speaker gives clues about her job, but without giving too much away.

Well, when I saw the job in the paper, it said, 'Go out and meet people!' you know. So, I thought, 'Well, that'll be the job for me, really.' So I went out and I had a little look, and now I've got the job and I do like meeting people. But you're outdoors all day. You know, when the rain comes and it's downing it, you don't half get sore feet. People expect me to be fat and horrible and old and pokey and I'm not like that at all really. I mean, I understand their problems, you know. They come up to me and they say, 'Well, there's double yellow lines everywhere.' 'Well,' I say, 'I know it's difficult, I mean, what with the traffic jams and all that,' and I say, 'Well, I'll give you five minutes, just five minutes, love, and then you'll have to be off and on your way, all right?' And some of them think I'm a little Hitler, but I'm not.

1 use of pronouns
In line 7, 'they' refers to the drivers. Can you find some other examples of similar use of pronouns?

2 being imprecise
In line 10, 'five minutes' are to do what? The speaker doesn't state what the five minutes are for. Find other examples.

3 choice of words
The speaker gives clues by using words associated with traffic, such as 'yellow lines'. Find another example.

B Read the job description below.

I'm a chef. You only have to look at me to realize my problem. I'm always tasting the food I cook. I have very long working hours as I start around 11 a.m. and hardly ever get home before midnight. I never get fed up with cooking because I'm always inventing new recipes. Often the customers ask me to come into the restaurant to tell me how much they've enjoyed their meal. That makes it all worthwhile. By the way, my wife never lets me into the kitchen at home.

Remembering what you did in the previous exercise, rewrite this paragraph, trying to make his job less obvious.

Speaking

A Look at the pictures above. Discuss with your partner the qualities you think a person would need to be successful in each job.

B What aspects of a job would give you most satisfaction? Discuss with your partner and arrange the following in your order of preference.

making money	variety in your work	challenge
meeting people	social status	being your own boss
helping others	security	opportunity to travel

7 Plain sailing

Listening

It is the last day of a week's sailing course. All the participants are expected to take a test to prove their ability to sail a boat competently. Each person has a sketch map on which to draw in the course. Listen to the instructor giving the directions, and draw in the course on the map below.

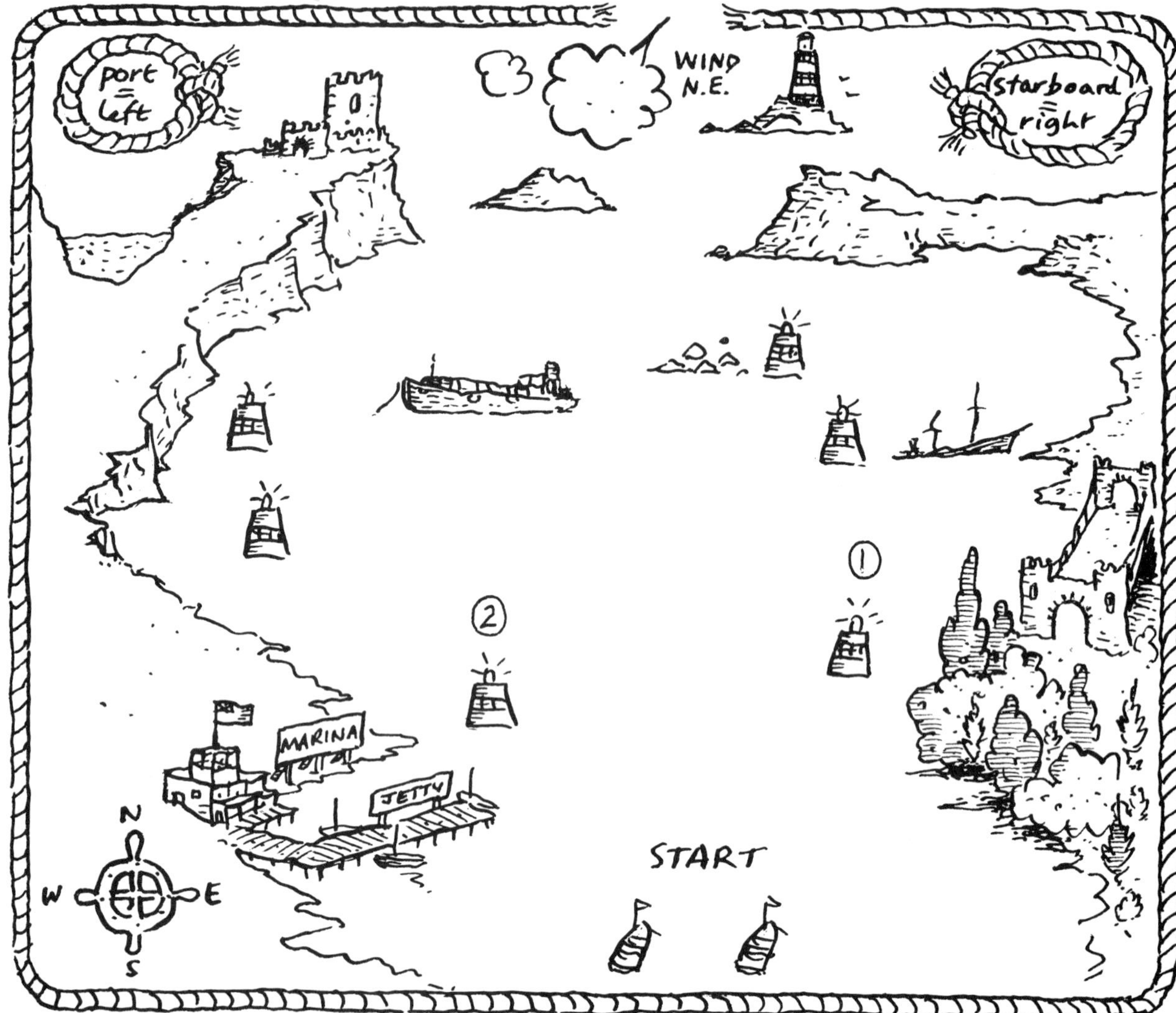

Practice

A Below are definitions of words the instructor uses that have to do with boats and water. Listen to the recording again and find the words.

1 river mouth
2 regular rise and fall in the level of the sea
3 small motor-boat used on rivers and lakes
4 floating secured object used as a marker to warn boats
5 landing place for boats
6 boat that has been destroyed
7 large, flat-bottomed boat used for carrying goods on rivers and canals
8 tall tower which has a powerful light to warn and guide ships

B Find four expressions the sailing instructor uses to remind students what they must and must not do.

1 . . . your life-jackets
2 . . . as you go round the buoy
3 . . . that a boat on a starboard tack has right of way
4 . . . or you might end up one yourself

C Find two words the instructor uses that mean *go towards*.

1 . . . back to the wood
2 . . . for the wood

Speaking

You are in charge of a group of young people on an outdoor pursuits course. Today they are to be tested on their ability to read a map and follow instructions accurately. Read the country code below, then draw a route on the sketch map. Describe your route to a partner, making sure to draw his/her attention to the relevant points in the country code. Your partner should trace the route on his/her map. Check the answer, then change roles.

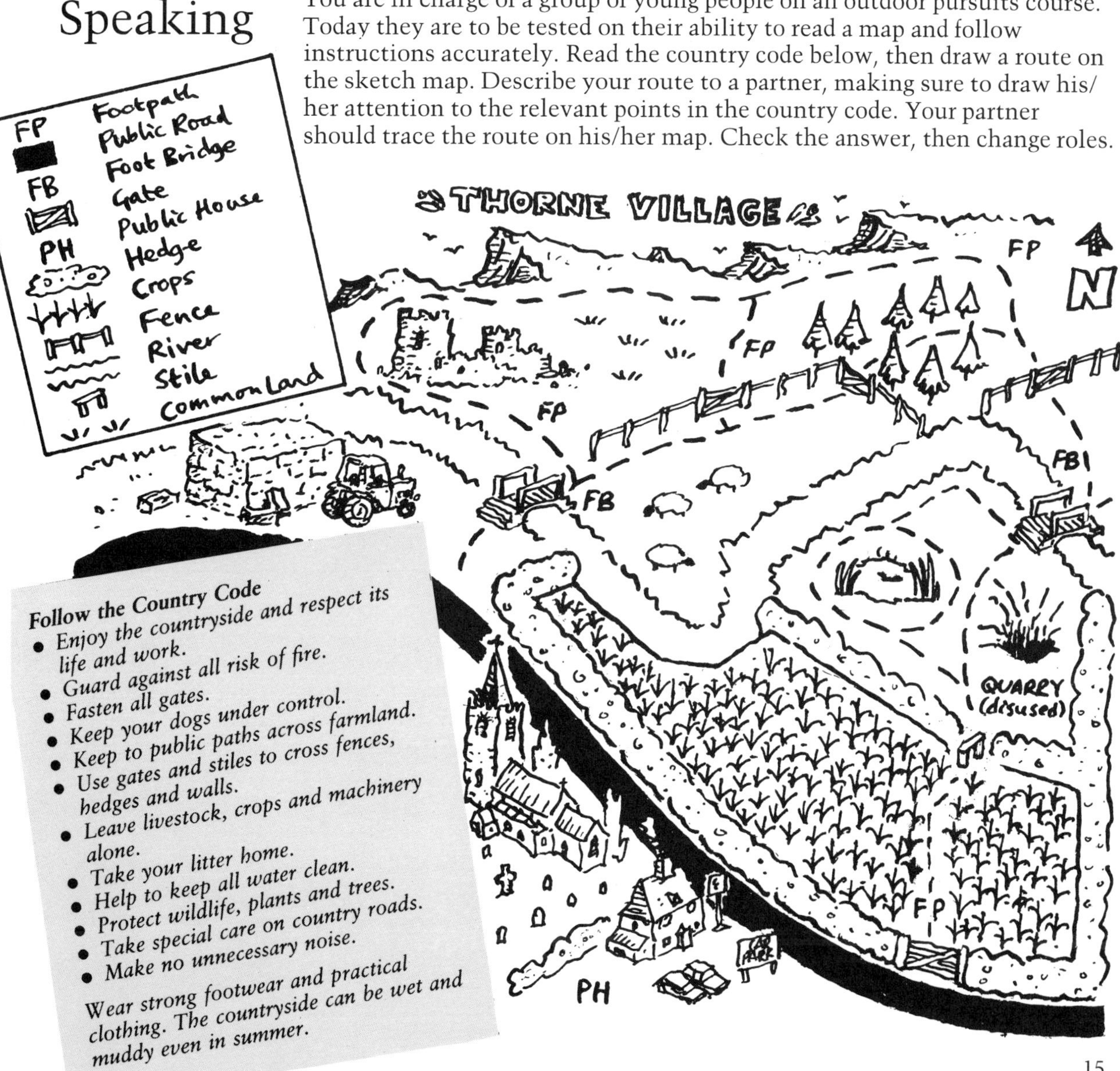

Follow the Country Code

- *Enjoy the countryside and respect its life and work.*
- *Guard against all risk of fire.*
- *Fasten all gates.*
- *Keep your dogs under control.*
- *Keep to public paths across farmland.*
- *Use gates and stiles to cross fences, hedges and walls.*
- *Leave livestock, crops and machinery alone.*
- *Take your litter home.*
- *Help to keep all water clean.*
- *Protect wildlife, plants and trees.*
- *Take special care on country roads.*
- *Make no unnecessary noise.*

Wear strong footwear and practical clothing. The countryside can be wet and muddy even in summer.

8 Till death us do part

Listening

In this recording, three women talk about marriage in their cultures. Usha, who speaks first, is from India, Hanne is from Denmark, and Lea from Brazil. Read the notes below which were made by a research student, then listen to the recording. Find the words to complete the notes.

Attitudes towards marriage in:

India:

Most marriages ...., but girl can .... Weddings v. ....; size depends on groom's .... in society. Even v. poor man has .....guests. Bride's parents meet all wedding .... Divorce ...., but v. ......

Brazil:

Marriage still a strong .... among middle and upper classes. Poor people just ...., and then .... Nowadays, wedding expenses .... Traditionally, ... parents responsible. Divorce possible since ...., but people only allowed to re-marry ......

Denmark:

Until recently, most people just .... together, and didn't bother to .... This presented legal problems when couple ...., so now marriage becoming more .... again. Ceremony - simple .... wedding or .... office. Usually paid for by .... and/or ....

Practice

A Because the discussion is informal, the speakers use a number of phrasal and prepositional verbs. For example, at the beginning, Hanne says that in Indian marriages the partners are *picked out* by their parents. She could have used the more formal *chosen*. Below are some of the phrasal and prepositional verbs the speakers use, but they are incomplete. Listen to the discussion again to find the missing particles.

	verb	meaning
1	to put ...	to unite
2	to work ...	to be successful
3	to go ...	to continue
4	to hang ...	to wait aimlessly
5	to depend ...	to relate to
6	to move ...	to begin to share a house
7	to split ...	to separate
8	to live ...	to share a house as husband and wife

B Look at the words below which have to do with weddings in Britain. Use your dictionary to check any words you do not know, then label the picture and complete the newspaper announcement.

people	**things**	**events**
clergyman	train	honeymoon
bridegroom	headdress	reception
bride	veil	ceremony
bridesmaid(s)	bouquet	
best man	church	

WEDDING ANNOUNCEMENT

Miss Sharon Jane Griffiths, of School Road, Leafield, was ... to Mr Colin Weeks of London at St Mary's ..., Leafield. The ... parents are Mr and Mrs John Griffiths, of Leafield, and the ... is the son of Mr Daniel Weeks and the late Mrs Weeks.

The ... ... was Mr Julian Weeks, and the ... was attended by ... Tracey Weeks and Julie Hicks. The ... was conducted by Rev David Wise and the ... was held at Leafield Village Hall. The newlyweds are spending their ... in the Canary Islands.

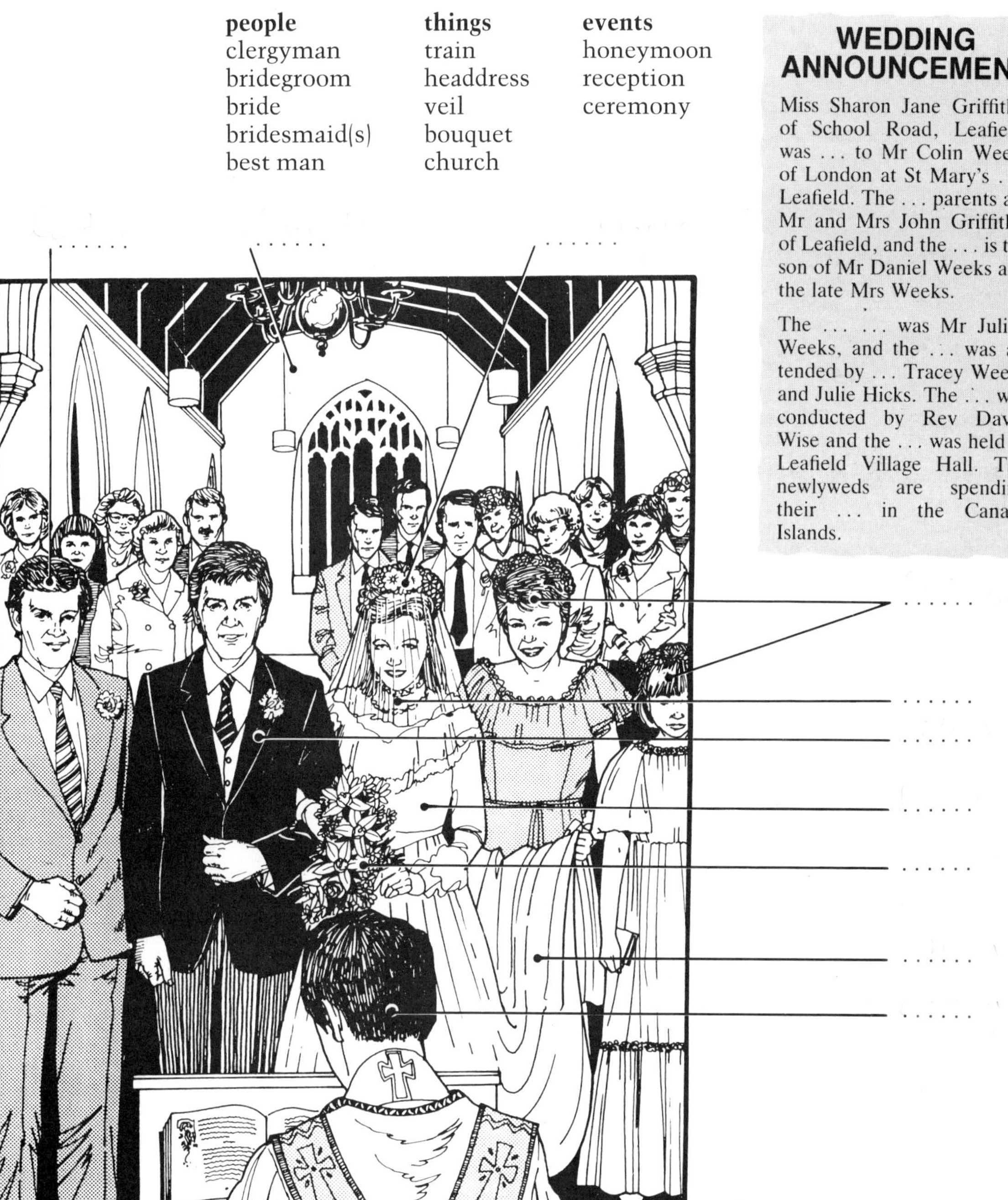

Speaking

Discuss the differences between marriages in India, Denmark and Brazil, and explain to your group how they compare to your own country's customs.

9 Another country

Listening

A Read the questions below, then listen to Berresford Lewis talking about his life in Britain, in 1985. Draw a line linking the relevant date to the event in Berry's life. The first one has been done for you as an example.

1932	is caretaker at college
1960	left British Leyland
1971	left St Vincent
1980	born
1985	left bakery

B In the box provided, mark (T) for true, (F) for false and (N) for no information for the following statements.

1 ☐ Berry regularly works in the evening.
2 ☐ Berry liked England as soon as he arrived there.
3 ☐ Berry applied for a job in Oxford from the West Indies.
4 ☐ Berry was made redundant by British Leyland.
5 ☐ Berry lives some distance from his present job.
6 ☐ Berry sells cosmetics in a shop.
7 ☐ Berry is married.
8 ☐ Berry has two children.

C In the boxes provided, tick (√) those tasks which Berry's caretaking job involves.

1 ☐ redecorating rooms
2 ☐ selling cosmetics
3 ☐ seeing to the needs of the lecturers
4 ☐ helping with the staff nursery
5 ☐ locking and unlocking doors

D Tick (√) the qualities which *you* think apply to Berry.

1 ☐ charming
2 ☐ shy
3 ☐ unsociable
4 ☐ lazy
5 ☐ talkative
6 ☐ generous
7 ☐ good-humoured
8 ☐ genial

Practice

A Listen to the recording again, paying particular attention to the interviewer's questions. Look at the exercise below, and find the words to complete the sentences.

1 What do you . . . do?
2 So you work shifts, . . .?
3 And when . . . you first . . . to England?
4 And how did you find . . . to England?
5 . . . did you come to Oxford?
6 So what did you do when you first . . . then?
7 . . . you . . . a job to come to?
8 . . . your first job?
9 And why did you . . . there?
10 You live just round the corner, . . .?
11 I hear that you sell cosmetics there too. . . . rather unusual, . . .?
12 . . . do you . . . sell it to them?
13 So you . . . do any demonstrations, or anything like that?
14 So how long . . . doing that then?
15 . . ., you're helping her to sell?

B Below are some of the types of questions the interviewer uses. For each type, find one more example.

1 'Wh-' questions (*who, what, why, when, where* and *how*) in the simple present:
So how do you actually sell it to them? (Q12)

2 'Wh-' questions in the simple past:
What did you do when you first came then? (Q6)

3 Tag questions:
That's rather unusual, isn't it? (Q11)

4 Questions with statement structure:
So really, you're helping her to sell? (Q15)

Speaking

Student A
You are a journalist covering the 1988 Presidential nominations in the USA. You have been granted an interview with Georgina Romoli, a strong contender for the Democratic nomination. Read her bio-data below, and decide on the areas you would like to question her about. Then interview her.

Georgina Romoli

Born in Kansas City in 1936. One of five children of Italian immigrant parents. Strong Catholic family. Father died when she was eight. Mother factory worker (clothing industry) - paid for Georgina's education.
1959 graduated from Columbia University.
Worked as high school teacher in Kansas City while studying law at night school.
1961, before graduating from law school, married property developer Ernest Chiaro. He provided financial backing for her political career.
Had three children.
1979 elected as Democratic Member of Congress for the borough of King's, Kansas City.
Vice Presidential candidate for 1984 Presidential elections.
Democratic ticket failed to win.
Regarded as strong contender for Democratic Presidential nomination in 1988. Strong on domestic policy but inexperienced in foreign affairs.

Student B
You are Georgina Romoli, a strong contender for the Democratic Presidential nomination. Study the bio-data above, and fill in some of the biographical gaps in order to prepare for your interview with a foreign journalist. Think about the issues listed below.

your role as representative of women (53% of voters in the USA)
how your career has developed
the experience you already have that would fit you for the job
the further experience you need to convince voters of your competence
your social and religious background
your husband
your children

10 Local government

Listening

You will hear part of a lecture on the organization of local government in England and Wales. Listen to the recording and complete the chart below.

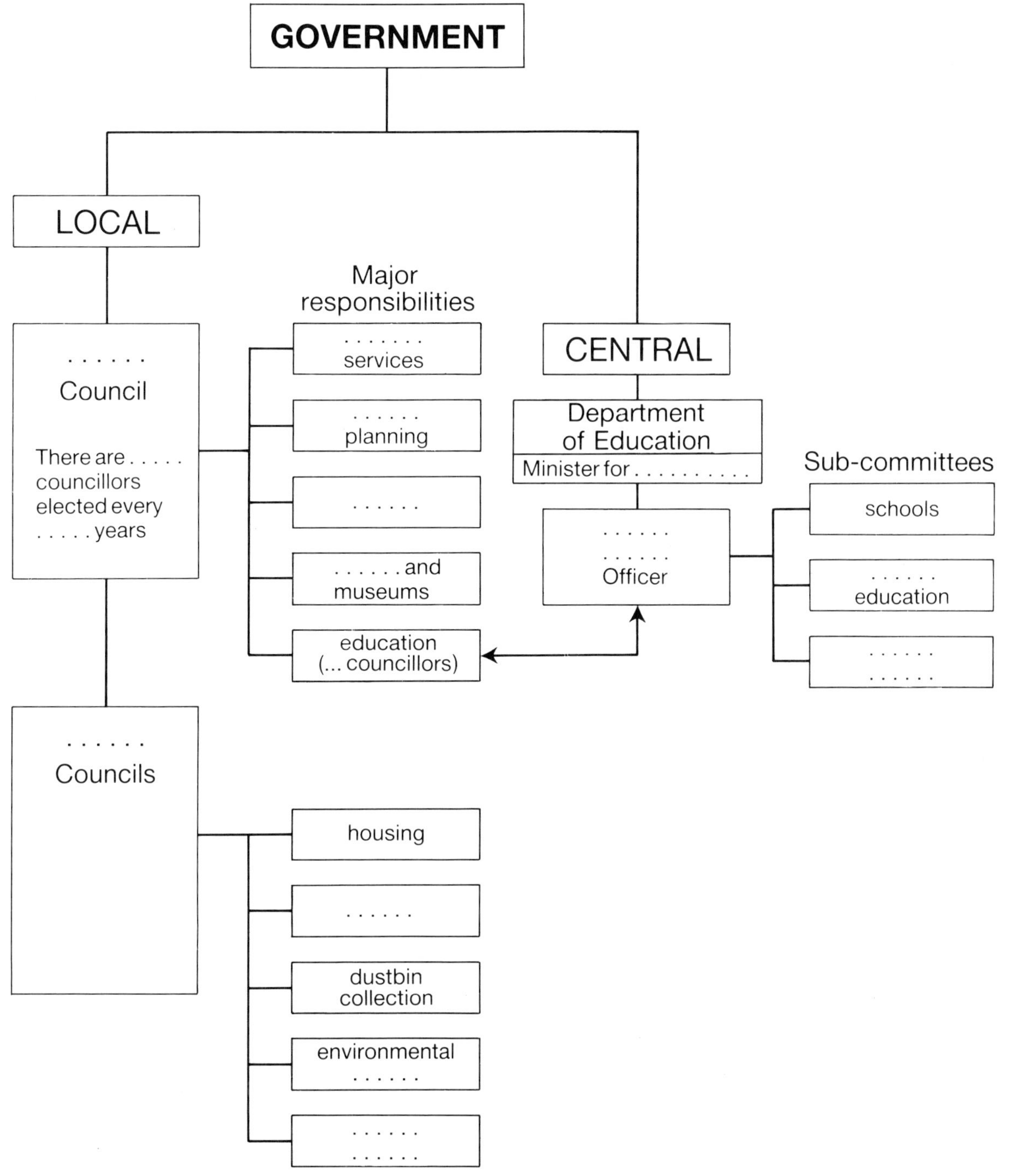

Practice

A A lecturer usually begins by making a general statement, and often follows this with an example. Some ways of linking a statement and an example are listed below.

such as
as shown by
as demonstrated by
for example (e.g.)
a case in point

Listen to the recording again and find the words the speaker uses in the sentences below to introduce examples.

1 If I . . . of Oxfordshire.
2 . . . they are building an ice rink in the middle of the city.
3 If we . . . about the question of education.
4 I think this . . . the idea of local government in the best way possible.
5 If we . . . of Oxfordshire again.
6 If I . . . of some of the structure.

B Imagine you were at the lecture. Prepare some questions for the lecturer on points you did not understand fully or you want to know more about. Remember: ask politely, correctly and precisely.

Speaking

Talk to your partner about education in his/her country. Find out about the following areas and try to get your partner's opinion on them.

the role of the government
whether education is free for everyone
starting and leaving ages
pre-school facilities
types of schools for different age-groups
exam systems
curriculum
streaming and mixed-ability classes
pupil power

11 Spot the sport

Listening

A Listen to the recording of five short extracts all relating to different sports and decide which of the following each one is. Fill in the appropriate letter in the top row of boxes.

a sports commentary
b conversation
c speech
d announcement
e broadcast interview
f news broadcast

B Listen to the recording again and identify each sport. Select your answers from the list below. Fill in the appropriate letter in the bottom row of boxes.

extract 1	extract 2	extract 3	extract 4	extract 5
e	f	b	e	a
wind-surfing	cricket	football	tennis	show-jumping

g basket ball
h rowing
i athletics
j cricket
k football
l horse-racing
m hockey
n tennis
o wind-surfing
p show-jumping
q table-tennis
r swimming

Practice

A Listen to the fifth recording again and pay particular attention to the verbs. Find the words to complete the transcription below, which starts about halfway through the recording. What are the two tenses that are contrasted?

She . . . the wall – oh, and they . . . . She, she . . ., she . . . a brick but it . . ., oh! And another tight turn – and . . . the last – oh dear! She . . . that completely wrong.

B Listen to the third recording again. Find the two different tenses that are contrasted and give two examples of each.

Speaking

DRAMA ON CENTRE COURT

Yesterday, Wimbledon's Centre Court was once again the centre of controversy. The capacity crowd rose to their feet to take the part of petite Lourdes Ferreira of Brazil, seeded number 15, pitted against New Zealand's white hot hope for the championship, number 4 seed, Valerie Hursthouse.

Problems started when 22 year old Miss Hursthouse served a double fault in a crucial game in the first set. A section of the crowd, which had clearly been rooting for the young Brazilian throughout the match, cheered exuberantly. Miss Hursthouse, seeded number one in her home country, swore loudly and complained in no uncertain manner to the umpire. She continued to do this every time the nimble Miss Ferreira won a hard-fought point.

For the crowd, the crunch came in the third set when Miss Hursthouse disputed a line call. Frustration and bad temper exploded as Miss Hursthouse hurled her racquet at her startled opponent, who narrowly escaped a blow. Boos and hisses rang from the usually well-mannered Wimbledon crowd, with individuals rising to their feet and demanding that the umpire stop the match. The Duchess of Kent, watching from the Royal Box, looked more than disconcerted at the uproar. Miss Hursthouse was eventually led sobbing from the court by her coach, Andrea Spanberg, and a bewildered Miss Ferreira packed up her racquets to the encouraging cheers of the crowd.

Student A
You have read the report on the Wimbledon match, and know that your friend was among the spectators there. Question him/her about it.

Student B
You were present at the incident outlined in the article. Talk to your partner about the experience.

12 Eccentrics

Listening

This is a conversation between two friends, Helen and Carole, who are chatting about four eccentrics they have met or seen. Look at the pictures carefully. Listen to the recording and put a tick (√) in the box beside each of the four people who are described.

Practice

A Read through the exercises below, then listen to the recording again. Find two ways Helen says she remembers the old lady well.

1 I had . . . of her.
2 I always . . . of her.

B Find two phrases Helen uses to say how much she liked the people she is describing.

1 I really . . . .
2 The character . . . .

C When Helen is talking about what the old lady did in the past, she uses the structure *used to*, e.g. *she used to ride a tricycle.* Carole uses a different structure for the same concept, when describing the habits of the woman in the British Museum. Find the structure Carole uses.

Speaking

A Describe an interesting relative of yours to a partner. Consider the following points:

looks
behaviour
personality
interests
any particular incident you associate with that person

B The following kind of rhythmic and humorous poem is known as a limerick. Read it aloud, paying careful attention to the stress.

There wàs an old màn of Perù
Who drèamt he was èating his shòe.
He wòke in the nìght
In a tèrrible frìght,
And fòund it was pèrfectly trùe.

Now make up a limerick of your own. It can be as silly as you like. Begin with one of the sentences below.

- There was a young girl of Hong Kong . . .
- There was a young man called Bright . . .
- There once was a man called Ted . . .

13 Dr Norton's surgery

Listening

This is a telephone conversation between a secretary and a doctor's receptionist in a health centre. Listen to the recording and complete the message below from the secretary to her boss.

MEMORANDUM TO .... FROM ....Angela..........

Subject .... Date ....23rd March..........

Arranged appointment re .... vaccination for ....

at .... with Dr .... (Dr .... ill).

Remember to take .... Cost: ....

Signature ....Angela..........

Practice

In a formal context, we often have to be outwardly polite, although we may be feeling annoyed or impatient. Read the thoughts in the bubbles and then listen to the recording again. Match up what the secretary or receptionist is thinking with what she actually says. Put the number in the appropriate bubble.

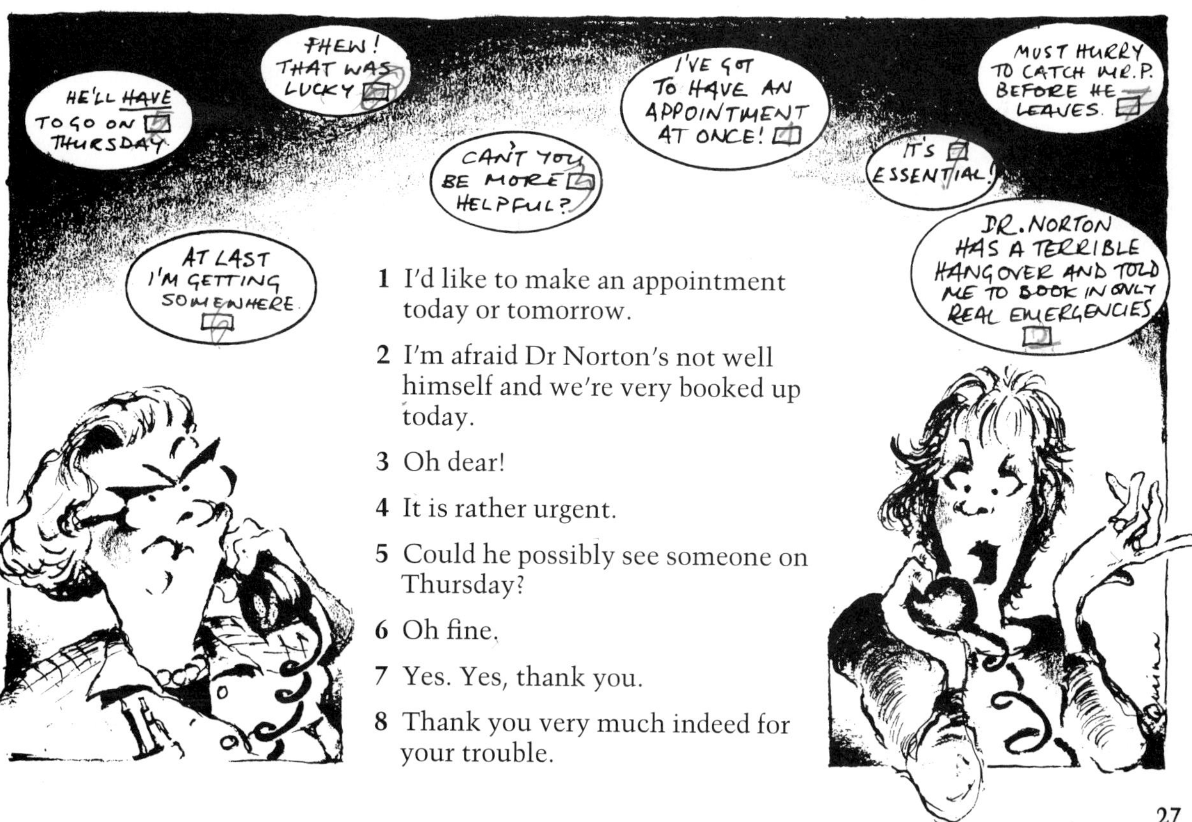

1 I'd like to make an appointment today or tomorrow.

2 I'm afraid Dr Norton's not well himself and we're very booked up today.

3 Oh dear!

4 It is rather urgent.

5 Could he possibly see someone on Thursday?

6 Oh fine.

7 Yes. Yes, thank you.

8 Thank you very much indeed for your trouble.

Speaking

With a partner, act out a dialogue based on the thoughts below between a secretary and her boss. Before you start, consider the relationship between the secretary and her boss, that a favour is being asked, and the kind of language each would use. The secretary should be very polite in order to get what she wants, but should not tell her boss everything. For example, she would probably say, 'I have a family problem', rather than, 'I want to see my boyfriend'.

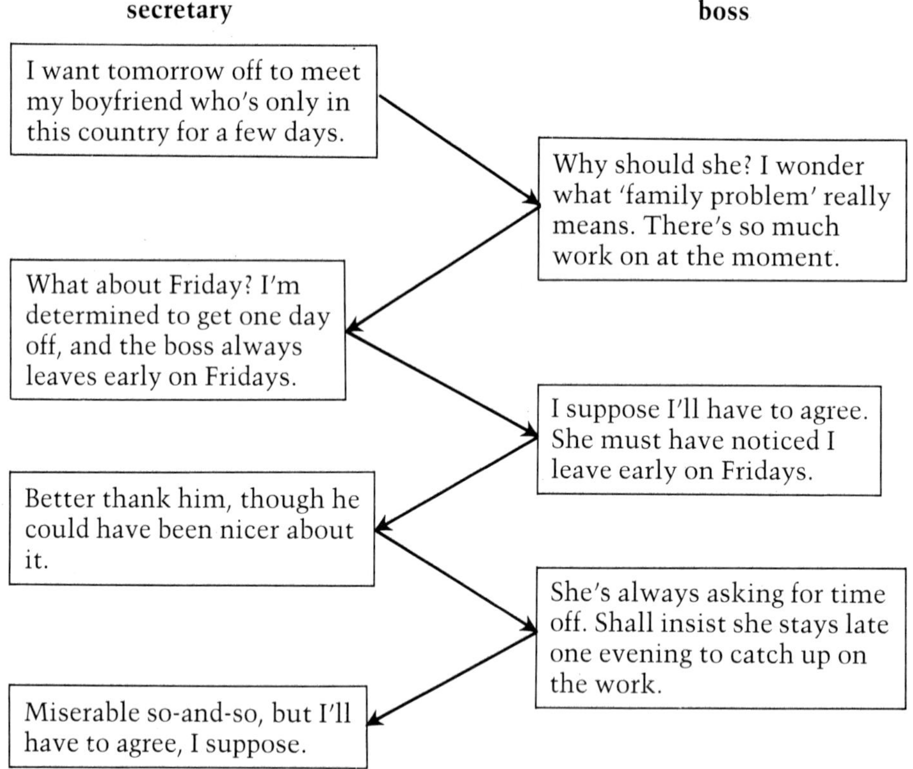

secretary
boss
I want tomorrow off to meet my boyfriend who's only in this country for a few days.
Why should she? I wonder what 'family problem' really means. There's so much work on at the moment.
What about Friday? I'm determined to get one day off, and the boss always leaves early on Fridays.
I suppose I'll have to agree. She must have noticed I leave early on Fridays.
Better thank him, though he could have been nicer about it.
She's always asking for time off. Shall insist she stays late one evening to catch up on the work.
Miserable so-and-so, but I'll have to agree, I suppose.

14 After a fashion

Listening

In this recording, two guides who work in a costume museum are showing a group of visitors around. They are describing costumes from four different periods. Put a tick (√) in the top box provided, for the costumes described. In the lower box, write the approximate date at which the clothes were worn.

Practice

A Listen to the recording again, and label as many parts of the costumes as you can. Use only the drawings mentioned in the recording. The more specialized words used are listed below.

parts of garments	supports	materials and decorations
overdress	frame	embroidery
underskirt	cage	lace
stomacher	pannier	trimming
headdress		feathers
frilled petticoat		muslin

B

1 Many verbs in English end in the suffix *-ate*. There are three in this recording. Listen again and try to find those verbs.

2 Look up the verb *imitate* in your dictionary and find the suffix to form the noun meaning *a person who imitates*. All verbs ending in *-ate* use the same ending. Form the nouns for the following:

a person who manipulates	a person who investigates
a person who demonstrates	a person who commentates

3 Using your dictionary to help you, find the endings of the following verbs. They end in *-ate*, *-ute*, or *-ish*.

deterior-	comm-	establ-	distingu-	poll-	evacu-	toler-	imit-
flour-	demol-	exec-	ref-	anticip-	disp-	implic-	dimin-

Speaking

A

It is the year 2050. You are a costume museum guide. Look at the photos below and describe the clothes worn in the mid 1980s.

B

In your group, discuss the significance of clothes. Think about the following areas.

wealth and fashion	dressing for work
developed and developing countries	clothes as a form of self-expression

15 At a loss for words

Listening

A In this recording, Alexandre and Carole are talking about the use of English words in French. According to them, these words fall into four categories. Listen to their conversation to complete the table below.

Categories	Example 1	Example 2	Example 3
1 No equivalent word in French	. . .	. . .	–
2 . . .	*speakerine* (means . . .)	. . . (means 'dinner jacket')	. . . (means 'pyjamas')
3 . . .	*building*	–	–
4 . . .	*parking*	–	–

B Answer the questions by ticking the correct alternative a, b, or c in the box provided.

1 Carole and Alex are probably at the

a ☐ airport.
b ☐ hairdresser's.
c ☐ dentist's.

2 When Carole says, 'Training means something quite different', she means

a ☐ 'training' has a related though different meaning in English.
b ☐ the French and English meanings are not related.
c ☐ 'training' means the opposite in English.

3 When Carole says that English words are snobbish in French, her voice tells us that she

a ☐ is surprised.
b ☐ disagrees.
c ☐ is impatient.

4 Carole thinks 'building' is an odd word to adopt because it

a ☐ is so hard to pronounce.
b ☐ has so many meanings.
c ☐ has no elegant connotations in English.

Practice

A

In informal conversation a speaker will often repeat points (his/her own or the other person's), in order to confirm and clarify what has been said. Listen to the recording again and find the words to complete the confirming statements in the table below.

Original statement	Confirming statement
1 There was a strong reaction against it	People . . .
2 We've got no word	It's often . . .
3 Snob value, I suppose	You . . .
4 It's such a mundane word	It sounds . . .

B

Most verbs in English have a related noun. For example, *to think* (verb), *a thought* (noun). Many verbs also have a related noun which means 'a person or thing that . . .' For example, *thinker*, a person who thinks.

Look at the words below that occur in the recording and find the related nouns and verbs to complete the chart. Use your dictionary to help you.

Verb	**Related noun**	**Related noun A person or thing that . . .**
think	a thought	a thinker (person)
1 laugh	1 . . . 2 . . .	–
2 . . .	an expression	–
3 . . .	. . .	an announcer (person)
4 . . .	a reaction	. . . (thing)
5 occur	. . .	–
6 . . .	imperialism	. . . (person)
7 . . .	an example	–
8 . . .	a distortion	. . . (person)
9 borrow	–	. . . (person)
10 . . .	a building	. . . (person)

Speaking

A In your group, discuss the following issues.

Are any foreign words used in your language? If so, what are they, and why do they occur?
Are the categories of words that are distinguished in the conversation relevant to your language?
Is there a strong reaction to foreign words by some people?

B Discuss the problems that occur when a single language, like English, is used for international communication.

16 Waiting in the wings

Listening

Read the questions below, then listen to the recording of a radio arts programme. A famous aging actress is being interviewed about her life and career by an inexperienced journalist. Answer the questions by ticking (√) the appropriate alternative, a, b, or c, in the box provided.

1 The play in which Dame Kitty first became famous was

a ☐ *The Rat Trap.*

b ☐ *Heartbreak House.*

c ☐ *The Nun's Tragedy.*

2 Dame Kitty

a ☐ took over Nelly Perry's part because Nelly Perry was drunk.

b ☐ broke her leg because she had taken over the lead from Nelly Perry.

c ☐ pushed Nelly Perry downstairs so she could take over her part.

3 Dame Kitty's autobiography was written by

a ☐ Alex Smart.

b ☐ a professional author.

c ☐ Dame Kitty.

4 Dame Kitty's father came from

a ☐ Morecambe.

b ☐ Hackney.

c ☐ Surbiton.

5 From the interviewer, we learn that Dame Kitty has been married to

a ☐ an actor.

b ☐ a solicitor.

c ☐ a doctor.

6 Dame Kitty had a good working relationship with

a ☐ Nellie Melba.

b ☐ Nelly Perry.

c ☐ Lester Guthlaxton.

7 When the interviewer says 'I beg your pardon?' he

a ☐ doesn't hear what Dame Kitty says.

b ☐ doesn't understand what Dame Kitty means.

c ☐ is contradicting Dame Kitty.

8 The interviewer says the name 'Shakespeare' in

a ☐ desperation.

b ☐ disgust.

c ☐ disbelief.

9 The interviewer says 'I think I just heard your five minute call'

a ☐ because he wants listeners to know that the interview is live.

b ☐ to shut Dame Kitty up.

c ☐ because he doesn't want Dame Kitty to miss her entrance.

10 'Many happy returns' means the interviewer

a ☐ hopes the play will be a financial success.

b ☐ is wishing Dame Kitty a happy birthday.

c ☐ hopes Dame Kitty will come back to the Theatre Royal, Morecambe many more times.

Practice

A Listen to the recording again, concentrating on the language the journalist uses to interrupt and guide the interview. Find the words for the gaps (. . .) in the following sentences.

1 **Dame Kitty** – but I'd just spent three months in a musical version of *The Seagull* so even then I –
☐ **Interviewer** . . . fate . . . and you took over the lead.
2 **Dame Kitty** Mark you , she hung on pretty hard to the bannisters.
☐ **Interviewer** . . . a little . . . how you came to take up a stage career.
3 **Dame Kitty** If you tell 'em your father was a respectable solicitor from Surbiton who –
☐ **Interviewer** . . . . Your first husband was a medical pioneer, I believe?
4 **Dame Kitty** Pour me another while you're at it.
☐ **Interviewer** . . . theatrical career, Dame Kitty –
5 **Dame Kitty** The director hardly ever took his eyes off Romeo, they were always rehearsing the bedroom scene without me.
☐ **Interviewer** . . . . Dame Kitty, what part do you look back on with most pleasure?
6 **Dame Kitty** I managed to sink my teeth into that pompous old lecher Sir Lester Guthlaxton.
☐ **Interviewer** . . . heard your five minute call.

B For each example above, put a, b, or c, in the boxes provided to show whether the journalist is trying to

a change the subject.
b keep the conversation moving.
c bring the conversation back to a previous topic.

Speaking

A Television chat shows, in which a regular interviewer talks to a well-known personality, are very popular in Britain. In your group, discuss why this is, and what qualities and practical facilities the host/hostess of a chat show needs.

B

Student A
You are a chat show presenter. Prepare twenty questions to ask a famous film star, but be willing to depart from your question list if the situation demands it. You must therefore listen carefully to your guest's replies.

Student B
You are a famous film star. Note down the main events in your professional and personal life, in preparation to be interviewed on a television chat show.

17 Jobspot

Listening

A This recording is from a local radio programme that is broadcast daily and gives out information about job vacancies. Listen to the recording and complete the chart below. Put a tick (√) where appropriate, or (N) for no information. Some of the information has already been filled in for you.

Job	Full-time	Part-time	Experience			Age	Pay	Hours
			essential	useful	not necessary			
hairdresser	√					...	...	Monday–Friday ... Saturday ...
...						...	£ ... per hour	...
...						...	£ ... per hour	Monday ... Tuesday–Saturday ... Sunday ...
shorthand typist						...	...	...
...					√	...	£ ... per week	...

B Listen to the item on the gardener's job again. Look at the chart below and complete it with the following information:

1 two tasks the gardener will be expected to do
2 two qualities the gardener should have

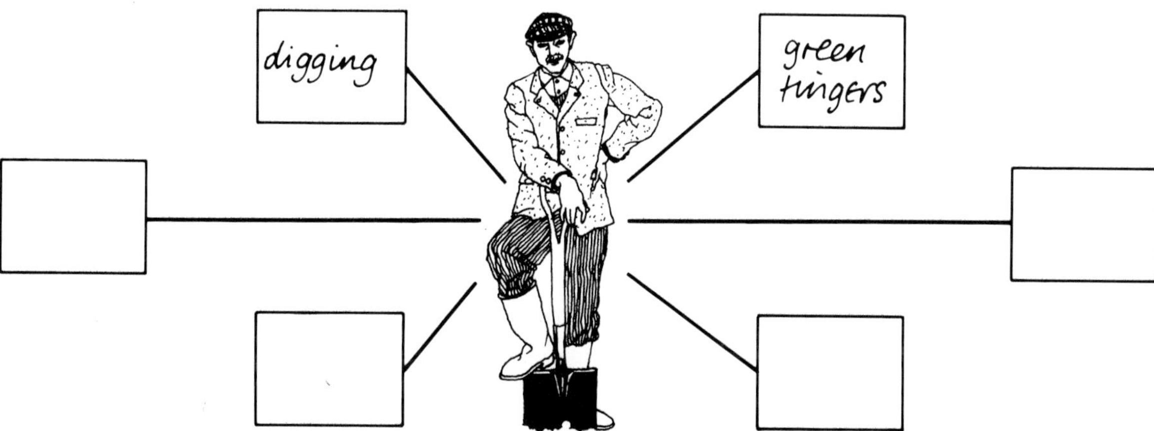

Practice A

1 The gardening equipment below can be used for either digging, potting or watering. Join the tool to the correct box.
2 Name the tools. Some clues have been given.

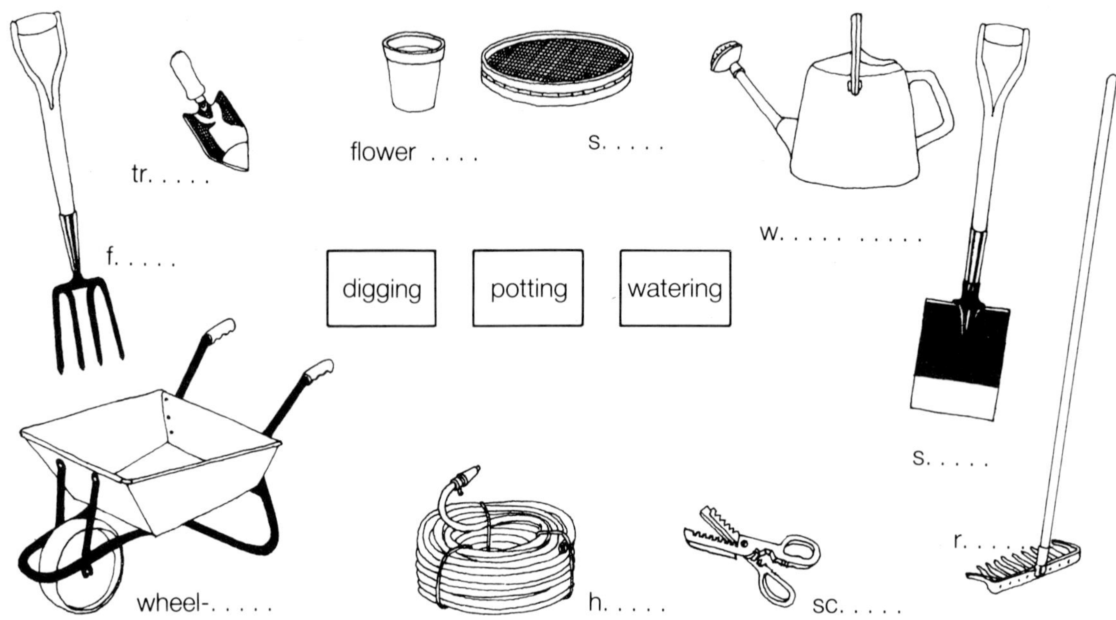

B

In your dictionary, look up the words below that you do not know. There are four sets of four words. Each set is associated with a different job. Find each set, and the job associated with it.

saw	syringe	thermometer	bandage
plane	hammer	flex	screwdriver
spanner	wrench	jack	gauge
fuse	plug	stethoscope	chisel

C

1 Find an expression meaning *to like*.
2 Find two expressions the speaker uses to make a suggestion.

Speaking

With a partner, write a 'jobspot' so that each of the following people could apply for at least one position. Keep the style friendly and informal, as in the recording.

An 18-year-old girl interested in working with computers.
A 42-year-old redundant factory worker willing to do anything.
A 21-year-old graduate who can type and drive.
A 30-year-old man who has done a variety of jobs, is interested in working with people, but has no formal qualifications.

18 Help!

Listening

Liza receives a phone call from a friend. Listen to her side of the conversation and answer the questions below. Tick (√) the alternative which seems to you the most likely, in the box provided.

1 a ☐ The caller is offering to do Liza a favour.
  b ☐ The caller is asking Liza to do him/her a favour.

2 a ☐ The caller is going away on holiday.
  b ☐ The caller is going away on business.

3 a ☐ The caller wants her to look after a lot of things.
  b ☐ The caller wants her to look after a few things.

4 a ☐ The caller is asking Liza to pick some friends up from the station.
  b ☐ The caller wants Liza to look after a pregnant animal.

5 When Liza asks, 'Why do you keep them?'
  a ☐ she is indicating that she is not very happy with the arrangement.
  b ☐ she is thinking of keeping them herself.

6 When Liza says, 'I won't have to worry about it', she is referring to
  a ☐ food.
  b ☐ work.

7 a ☐ The caller is going to bring round a lot of carrots.
  b ☐ The caller is going to bring round a sack of fresh vegetables.

8 The conversation is about looking after
  a ☐ children.
  b ☐ rabbits.
  c ☐ cats.

9 Guess whether the person Liza is talking to is
  a ☐ male.
  b ☐ female.

Practice

A Liza commits herself wholeheartedly to the proposal at the outset of the conversation when she says, 'Just anything you want.' As the plan unfolds, she has to withdraw slightly and express her reservations. How does she do this? Listen to the recording again and find the words to complete the sentences below.

1 . . ., how many of them are there?
2 Oh no! Why, I'm . . . now.
3 Why, that's just a little too many. I mean, oh I don't . . . .
4 Well, I sincerely hope not. I mean, I'm . . . thing.

B Liza repeatedly uses three expressions to keep her side of the conversation moving, and to give her time to think. One of them is *well*. Find the other two.

Now listen to the full version of the conversation and compare it to the answers you chose.

Speaking

Student A
Ask a friend to look after your house or flat while you are away. There are a number of things you want your friend to do for you, but break the news gently. Some of the things you must include are listed below.

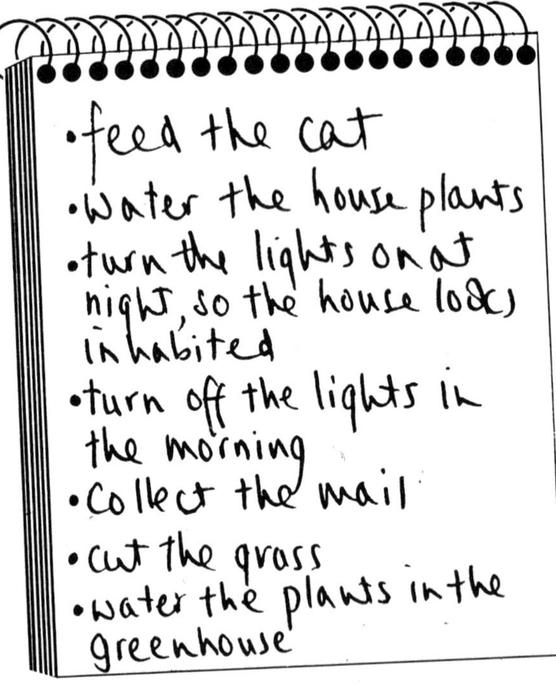

•feed the cat
•water the house plants
•turn the lights on at night, so the house looks inhabited
•turn off the lights in the morning
•collect the mail
•cut the grass
•water the plants in the greenhouse

Student B
A good friend of yours who you want to please, will ask you a favour. Agree readily. There may turn out to be a number of snags, so you will need to withdraw gradually. Play for time and express your reservations. You will probably reach a compromise.

19 Coping

Listening

A This recording is of a conversation between Teresa and Pauline, the mother of a mentally handicapped boy, about the problems and pleasures of bringing him up. Read through the questions before listening to the recording, then tick (√) the correct alternative a, b, or c, in the box provided.

1 Pauline
- **a** ☐ does not like talking about Andrew.
- **b** ☐ is willing to talk a little about Andrew.
- **c** ☐ is happy to talk about him.

2 When Andrew was born, the family
- **a** ☐ knew at once he was mentally handicapped.
- **b** ☐ knew immediately there was something wrong with him.
- **c** ☐ had no idea he was mentally handicapped.

3 The most frustrating thing for Andrew is that people
- **a** ☐ don't talk to him.
- **b** ☐ find his speech difficult to understand.
- **c** ☐ talk to him when he doesn't want them to.

4 Pauline's greatest worry is that
- **a** ☐ Andrew might be attacked by hooligans.
- **b** ☐ he will never be able to live on his own.
- **c** ☐ people may realize he is mentally handicapped when they see him.

B In the boxes provided, mark (T) for true or (F) for false for the following statements.

1 ☐ Andrew can dress himself very well.
2 ☐ Andrew is a sociable person.
3 ☐ Andrew plays some sports.
4 ☐ Andrew can travel around by himself.

Practice

A The sentences below have been taken from the recording but the words in italics substituted for the original words. Listen to the recording again and find the original word or phrase in the conversation.

1. He's mentally *subnormal*.
2. I'm sorry. I *didn't realize*.
3. I don't mind talking about him *at all*.
4. We didn't know what it was *at the beginning*.
5. His intelligence is very *limited*.
6. He does have a lot of difficulty in *speaking*.
7. That must be very *disturbing* for him.
8. He *manages* very well.
9. What does he *like* doing?

10 He helps in the house *a bit*.
11 He loves to play snooker *for instance*.
12 How well can he *take care of* himself?
13 He'll put on two pairs of socks *rather than* one.
14 *Yet*, he can wash and dress himself.
15 Can he get about *by himself*?
16 He wouldn't be able to ask *for directions*.
17 Nobody would *be sure*.
18 One never really stops having *worries*.
19 He has a sort of *talent* for happiness.
20 Everybody's much more understanding about things *today*.

B In this conversation Pauline does most of the speaking. Teresa's role is to show Pauline that she is interested to hear about Andrew and wants her to continue talking. Making polite 'noises' is something you do automatically in your own language, and you may not be aware of what you actually do or say.

On the tape you heard Teresa using some of the 'noises' listed below for signifying her continued interest. Listen to the first part of the recording again and find the appropriate response to complete the conversation.

uhuh, oh dear, ah yes, oh, really, goodness, what a pity, mm, I see, no

1 **Pauline** She's trying to be an opera singer.
Teresa . . .

2 **Pauline** He's mentally handicapped.
Teresa . . .

3 **Pauline** It's Down's syndrome.
Teresa . . .

4 **Pauline** It means that people sort of have some understanding that there's something wrong.
Teresa . . .

5 **Pauline** He helps in the house a certain amount.
Teresa . . .

Speaking

Look at the picture opposite and discuss in your group the problems disabled people face. Consider the following points:

how individuals can help
how the community can help
ways in which public facilities can be made more convenient for disabled people

“As far as I’m concerned it’s neither public nor convenient.”

THE SPASTICS SOCIETY

It’s not that people don’t care, it’s just that they don’t think.

20 And later today

Listening

This recording is taken from a radio station. The announcer, with a few minutes to spare before the next part of the programme, gives the listeners some information about programmes for the rest of the morning.

Below is a transcription made by an audio-typist. She has made a number of mistakes. In some places she realized and put a question mark (?) or an omission sign (∧). Read the transcript carefully, noting places where you think a mistake might have been made, then listen to the recording and make the necessary corrections.

Studio production was by Brendan Donavan, and the editors were
Francis Barnes and Eric Newton. Before the nine o'clock news, a
quick look at one of this morning's headlines. At five to nine
theirs ?Signs Tomorrow with Jean Hook, and it's followed by
The Wall Around Us, when we learn about antipodean curiosities,
how the platypus wore his spure and why kangaroos are called
joeys. That is Babies of the Pouch at nine thirty. After Tale
at Ten, the first in a new ∧ of theatrical profiles, with the
title Waiting in the ?Wind. And this morning Ray Keeling talks
to the ∧ old theatrical dame, Kitty Spurge.
(Excerpt)
?Former of Dame Kitty's colourful reminiscences, turn on at ten
fifty for Waiting in the Wind. Later at two minutes past
eleven, an examination of socialistic agricultural policis
world ∧ when the Spectrum ∧ presents Let them eat Coke.
Finally, at eleven forty nine, today is a concert, when the
Bognor Philharmonic, ∧ the baton of Wanda van Ek will be
bringing us Elgar Sea Songs sung by Evadne Butcher.

Practice

A Only ten of the words below occur in the recording. Put a tick (√) beside the ones you remember, then listen to the recording again to check your answers.

☐	production	scriptwriters	☐
☐	portraits	tune in	☐
☐	editors	introduces	☐
☐	serial	direction	☐
☐	studio	set	☐
☐	features	profiles	☐
☐	presents	series	☐
☐	switch on	highlights	☐
☐	credits	team	☐
☐	group	title	☐

B Each word in the first column above has a partner in the second. They do not necessarily mean the same thing, but would be found together. For example, both *production* and *direction* are aspects of making a programme. Link the word in the first column to its partner in the second. One has been done for you as an example. Use your dictionary to help you.

C The following nouns from Practice A all have a related verb. For example, *to direct* is the verb related to the noun *direction*. Use your dictionary to help you find the verbs related to the nouns below.

editors highlights serial portrait team production

Speaking

Read the passage below silently and then discuss with your partner what it is, where you would see/hear it, and where the information would come from. Underline the stressed words and then read it aloud for your partner to check.

Tower Bridge is closed until early on Monday morning, so use London Bridge or Blackwall Tunnel. In Kent, Maidstone town centre's closed because of a carnival. Avoid that if you're driving. As you've heard, there's been motor racing at Brand's Hatch today, so expect very heavy traffic on the A20 between Dartford and Wrotham as the crowds leave. If you are going tomorrow and you want to join the M25 from the M1, leave the M1 at junction 7, the St Alban's exit, take the M10, then the A405, and the A6 to the M25 which you can join at South Mimms at junction 23.

21 Fairground Dream

Listening

Read the lyrics to the pop song below. Try to work out what the missing words are, then listen to the recording and find the missing words. Each gap represents one word.

FAIRGROUND DREAM

The fair was in town for a couple of days
One midsummer . . . . . . with the sky . . . . . .
I . . . . . . among the sideshows
When . . . . . .! I saw this vision.

Tall and smiling with an easy . . . . . .
The sunlight . . . . . . on his long blond hair
I felt a . . . . . . emotion
I had to . . . . . in closer.

There was . . . . . with him
That I . . . . . see
But when I came . . . . . up to him
I . . . . . . speak.

I . . . . . . him the whole fair through
The caterpillar and the dodgems . . . . . .
Once close . . . . . . to touch him
I didn't have the . . . . . .

The . . . . . . it got, the less it felt real
I followed him onto the Ferris . . . . . .
We . . . . . . the trees together
In separate . . . . . . again, though.

I saw his car stop . . . . . . me
He rejoined the . . . . . .
But when I got out of my car
He was . . . . . . to be found.

I didn't stop . . . . . . till I knew he'd gone
The wheel was black against the setting . . . . . .
He'd gone, he'd gone for . . . . . .
My fairground . . . . . . was over.

by Michael Scannell

Practice

A Four verses of the song each have two lines that rhyme. The other three verses have lines that do not quite rhyme. Look at the words below, listen to the song again, and pair the words that rhyme by linking them with a line. Leave the words that do not rhyme. You should have four rhyming pairs at the end.

speak	real
days	through
found	hair
wheel	crowd
sun	see
air	ablaze
too	gone

B Look at the six words below. Each one rhymes with two words in the circle. Using your dictionary to help you, group the words together according to rhyme.

see speak crowd found gone sun

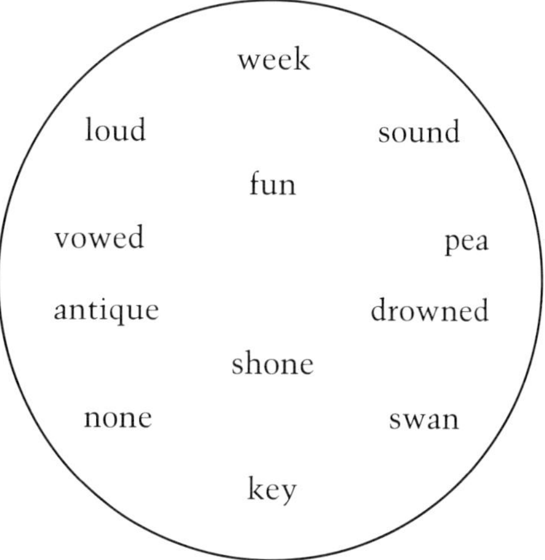

Speaking

In your group, discuss the following issues.

What are the ingredients of a successful pop song?
What are the qualities which produce an internationally famous pop star?
Why are some pop stars so wealthy?
Do you think that they deserve to earn so much?

22 What's on?

Listening

Every summer, Edinburgh, the capital city of Scotland, holds an international arts festival. In addition to the regular events, a great many other groups put on shows which are not part of the official festival. This is known as *The Fringe*.

Lizzie and Ben are in Edinburgh to go to as many of the events as they have time and money for. As there are about five hundred events, it is difficult to decide. They are in a pub discussing their plans for the following day. Look at the programme below, but do not read all the details. Only read the heavy print. Listen to the recording and find out where **Lizzie** decides to go. Where appropriate, put a tick (√) in the boxes provided on the programme.

THEATRE

☑ **BAHUMUTSI T.C. OF SOWETO, S.A.**
VENUE 35 Little Lyceum, Cambridge Street.
THE HUNGRY EARTH by Maishe Maponya. Excellent presentation of the history of S. Africa. Depicts the people's struggle against the system.
Aug 24–30 (not Sun.) 2.00 p.m. (3.20) £2.50

☑ **CAMBRIDGE VAIN EMPIRES**
VENUE 8 Celtic Lodge, Brodies Close, Lawnmarket.
THE TEMPEST by William Shakespeare. 'Extraordinary: a savage Tempest, a mad Tempest ... fired by primitive magic and tribal rites ...' *Theatre Times.*
Aug 23–Sept 10 (not Sun.) 3.35 p.m. (5.25) £1.80

☐ **OXFORD DRAMA PROGRAMMES**
VENUE 41 Masonic Lodge, 19 Hill Street.
TWELFTH NIGHT by William Shakespeare. International student company in new production from Oxford Festival.
Aug 23–27 12.45 p.m. (2.15) £2.50

☐ **URGENT THEATRE, OXFORD**
VENUE 132 St Patrick's Primary School.
HEARTBREAKERS. A young boy gropes his way through adolescence into manhood: it is a painful and tragic journey. Powerful treatment of the loss-of-innocence theme.
Aug 18–Sept 3 (not Sun.) 9.30 p.m. (11.00) £2.00

☐ **CAMBRIDGE UNIVERSITY THEATRE GROUP**
VENUE 12 Royal Overseas League, Princes St.
NEW ZONE WEST by Tony Lopez. Multi-media show incorporating lights, video, recorded sound and making and distributing artwork to the audience. An examination of the politics of art.
Aug 23–Sept 10 (not Sun.) Noon (12.45) £1.00

COMEDY

☐ **THEATRE WORKSHOP COMPANY**
VENUE 35 Little Lyceum, Cambridge Street.
ACCIDENTAL DEATH OF AN ANARCHIST by Dario Fo. Disguise, lunacy and good humour are the ingredients of this grotesque farce.
Aug 17–Sept 3 (not Sun.) 7.30 p.m. (9.30) £2.50
Sept 5–10 7.15 p.m. (9.15)

☐ **NEWSREVUE (STRODE-JACKSON)**
VENUE 7 Heriot Watt Theatre (Upstairs) Grindlay Street
NEWSREVUE 1983 Award winning satirical revue first seen on BBC 1. 'Brilliant'.
Aug 18–Sept 10 8.45 p.m. (10.15) £2.50

EXHIBITIONS

☑ **COLIN BAXTER**
VENUE 1 Old Assembly Close, by Fringe Office
NEW LANDSCAPE PHOTOGRAPHS. A new venue for this popular exhibition which has already achieved great success at home and abroad.
Aug 13–Sept 10 10.00 a.m.–5.30 p.m. Free

☐ **AMNESTY INTERNATIONAL**
VENUE 126 The Corner Stone, St John's Church
BOIAS FRIAS – images from Brazil. Two artists show drawings and water colours reflecting courage, stoicism and social satire. Mauricio Alvarez and Merlin Currie.
Aug 22–Sept 3 10.00 a.m.–7.00 p.m. (not Sun.) Free

MUSICALS

☐ **STUDIO THEATRE NEW YORK**
VENUE 44 Viewforth Centre, 104 Gilmore Place
YOU'RE A GOOD MAN, CHARLIE BROWN. Musical adaptation of Charles Shultz's popular cartoon strips. One of the United States' most successful musicals.
Aug 23–27 11.00 a.m. (12.30) £1.50

MIME

☐ **DAVID GLASS MIME**
VENUE 3 Assembly Rooms, George St.
THE WHITE WOMAN. Exciting new mime from one of the genre's leading exponents. Set to the dynamic music of Grace Jones.
Aug 17–27 2.00 p.m. (3.35) £2.50

ROCK, JAZZ, BLUES

☐ **MILLER AND FOWLER**
VENUE 61 Reid Concert Hall, Bristo Square
Local lads back in Edinburgh sounding better than ever. 'Dazzling', *Guitar* magazine.
Aug 21–Sept 3 (not Sun.) 8.00 p.m. (9.30) £2.00

☐ **TOM ROBINSON AND CREW**
VENUE 3 Assembly Rooms, 54 George St.
SON OF A GUN. A late night musical extravaganza with Robinson and crew.
Aug 17–28 00.15 a.m. (1.30) £3.00

Practice

A Listen to the recording again and find three ways of making suggestions.

1 . . . in the morning.
2 . . . that exhibition?
3 We . . . there for lunch.

B Find three ways in which Ben and Lizzie express agreement.

1 . . . . See you there at eleven.
2 . . . do that.
3 . . . go to that.

C Find two ways in which Ben indicates that he does not want to go to the mime.

1 Oh . . . mime!
2 I . . . mime.

Speaking

You and your boyfriend/girlfriend are on an English language course in Edinburgh during the festival. You have lessons every morning, but are free for the rest of the day. Your school runs a social programme and your course fee includes one coach outing, one theatre visit, and two sessions at the sports centre each week. Read through the week's programme below and discuss it with your partner. Decide which activities you want to attend, bearing in mind your individual interests, and that you have a limited amount of money.

	Monday	**Tuesday**	**Wednesday**	**Thursday**	**Friday**	**Saturday**	**Sunday**
Afternoon	Tennis 80p Swimming 60p Squash £1 available every day 2–9 p.m. Racquets and balls can be hired – details from Wendy. Now doing reduced rates on Wednesdays	Guided walk of the city to help you find your way around. Meet at reception at 2 p.m.	Visit to a whisky distillery. Coach leaves 2 p.m. outside main entrance. Tickets £4.00 in advance from Wendy (includes free tasting).	Visit to Edinburgh Castle. 12.30 p.m. – give names to Wendy. Pay at entrance (£1.50).	Visit to a woollen mill to see tartan being made. The mill has a shop where tartan is sold – good for souvenirs. Coach leaves 2 p.m. outside main entrance. Cost £5.00	All-day ramble in the Grampian Hills. Coach leaves 9 a.m. Tickets £5.00 in advance from Wendy (includes packed lunch).	Day trip to Loch Lomond. Coach leaves 8.30 a.m. Tickets £8.00 in advance from Wendy (includes 2-hour boat cruise).
Evening	Film on Edinburgh. Room 30 8 p.m. – Free Extra showing 6 p.m.	Visit to the Albion Theatre: *Mixed Doubles* (musical) 7.30 p.m. See Wendy for details. Cost £2.50	Disco Room 30 8 p.m. £2.00	Visit to Globe Theatre: *You're a good man, Charlie Brown* (musical comedy). 8 p.m. – details from Wendy. Cost £1.50	Visit to the world-famous Military Tattoo. Meet at reception 8.30 p.m. Cost £4.50	Shakespeare's *Twelfth Night* performed outside in Pavilion Gardens 7.45 p.m. Tickets £2.50 in advance from Wendy.	A visit to some typical old local pubs. Meet outside the White Horse, St James's Street 8 p.m. Free (excluding drinks!)

23 A Hollywood story

Listening

A In this recording, Blain, an actor, is telling a short, funny story about a friend of his. Below are the main points of the story, but in the wrong order. Listen to the recording and put the points in the correct order by placing the appropriate letter against the right number on the grid below. The first one has been done for you as an example.

a His agent rang him up.
b Tourists were allowed in the private areas.
c He went to Hollywood.
d Someone shouted that the tourists were coming.
e Blain has an Australian friend.
f All the tourists rushed in.
g What the tourists most wanted was to see a star.
h A tourist asked Blain's friend if he were a star.
i The stars would disappear.
j He was told he'd got a part in a Doris Day movie.
k On Blain's friend's first day he was having his lunch in the canteen.
l They were looking for a star.
m As soon as the tourists were seen approaching, the stars were warned.
n He was left alone in the canteen, apart from a couple of scene painters.
o Tours of the studio had been introduced to make some money.

1 *e*	**6**	**11**
2	**7**	**12**
3	**8**	**13**
4	**9**	**14**
5	**10**	**15**

B Listen to the recording again, and mark (T) for true or (F) for false for the following sentences.

1 ☐ Blain's friend's name was Bruce.
2 ☐ The film he had a part in was *Pillow Talk*.
3 ☐ One of the stars of the film was Frank Sinatra.
4 ☐ The tourists realized that the stars were warned that they had arrived.
5 ☐ Blain's friend was the only person in the canteen who could have been a star.
6 ☐ Blain's friend knew why everybody was leaving the canteen.
7 ☐ Blain gives the impression that the tourists were young and female.
8 ☐ The point of the story is that the tourist doesn't recognize Blain's friend, but thinks he might be a star.

Practice

A To tell a story successfully, the narrator has to give enough information for the listener to understand the background of the story. He/she also has to keep the narrative moving and explain points he/she thinks the listener will need clarified.

Blain uses three methods to clarify his points:

a repetition
b emphasis and slowing down
c giving a word or phrase with a similar meaning

Listen to the recording again and put a, b, or c, in the boxes provided for the method Blain uses to clarify the topics below.

1 ☐ *Pillow Talk*
2 ☐ Rock Hudson
3 ☐ Doris Day
4 ☐ coach tours
5 ☐ what they really wanted
6 ☐ their recreation
7 ☐ in the canteen
8 ☐ all the actors

B Blain shows that he is aware of his listener in two ways: firstly, by using words to signal that an explanation is coming, and secondly, by directing remarks at him/her.

1 Find the word(s) Blain uses when he wants to signal an explanation about a) *Pillow Talk* b) the studios losing money.
2 Find the words Blain uses to include the listener when explaining the film *Pillow Talk*.

C Blain employs a number of techniques to tell his story effectively. He uses a structure with *would* to express past habitual behaviour, which is typically used in narrative style (see Unit 12). Find examples of Blain's use of this structure.

Speaking

With a partner, make up a story (it need not be serious) in which each of the items pictured below is included. Consider the following points:

plot
background
use of direct speech for dramatic effect
the punchline

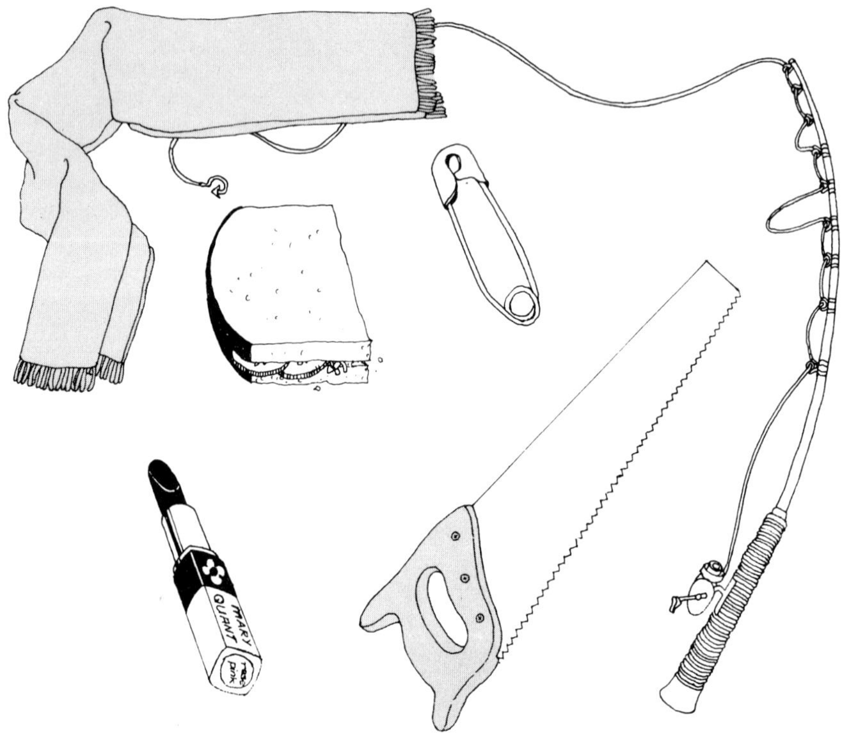

Answer key and notes

- The recordings include hesitations, repetitions, and switches of tense and grammar which are the usual features of authentic speech.

- Definitions given in the Language items refer only to meanings in context.

- Where appropriate, a model answer has been given for the Speaking section, but students and teachers should be aware that this is intended as a guide only. This occasionally applies to Practice also.

1 Ladies and gentlemen

The language used here is formal and polite, and the assumption is that the speaker and his listeners are of equal status. The announcements are of practical importance, so the delivery is clear and the essential information emphasized through stress, intonation and repetition. Note that not all the information is relevant to task B.
Accent: American

Tapescript

Ladies and gentlemen. If I could have your attention for a moment, please. I have the final notices for this final session of the conference. Now, first of all, I'd like to mention that the urban pollution session has been very popular, so we're moving the final discussion to Room 201. That's Room 201, which means that the domestic shelter session will be changed from Room 201 to Room 304. That's the domestic shelter session in Room 304. I hope everybody's got that.

Now, I have a notice here that you must return your keys to the Porter's Lodge before you leave. So anybody who has forgotten to bring them with you, please get them and return them before you leave. Thank you.

Turning now to your discussion records, I would like to see you return them to the session chairpeople by five o'clock this afternoon. That's 17.00 hours. Thank you.

Regarding coaches for the airport, er, they will be gathering outside the Kennedy Building at 3.30. That's, er, 15.30 hours. And there will be another one a little later than that at 15 hou . . . that's 17.15. That's 5.15. I'd like to ask you all to be there, ready for the buses, at least five minutes before the departure times, so we can all leave promptly and everybody will get home on time. Thank you.

I have particular messages for er, Dr Schap . . . Schapsinger and Dr Garbeldi and Dr Surinander. I'd like to ask you three – are you here? Dr Schapsinger, Dr Garbeldi? Yes. And Dr Surinander? I'd like to ask you to collect your reprints from the conference desk before you leave. Thank you.

Finally, I have a reminder from Dr Goldman of the Chicago Institute, that the sixth Annual Convention of P.E.S. will be held in Hawaii in October, er, 1986. I think you'll all be, er, interested in marking that date in your calendar. That's the sixth Annual Convention of P.E.S. October, '86. And I'd like anybody that's interested in that conference to leave your name at the conference desk. Thank you very much.

Ladies and gentlemen, I know it has been a very happy event for me, this conference, and I hope that you, too, have found it a happy and productive time. Thank you all for coming.

Language items

If I could have your attention for a moment . . . : a very polite request (an elliptical second conditional, '. . . I would be very grateful' has been suppressed)
chairpeople: a non-sexist alternative to 'chairmen'
reprints: copies of conference papers
I'd like anybody that's interested in that conference to leave your name: the speaker makes a grammatical switch in mid-sentence. He begins with the third person *anybody* but switches to the second person *leave your name* in the latter half of the sentence.

Listening

1 Final discussion of urban *pollution* will move to Room *201.*
2 Domestic *shelter* session will move to Room *304.*
3 Return *keys* to *Porter's* Lodge. ☑
4 Return discussion *records* to *session chairpeople* by *five o'clock.* ☑
5 First *coach* for airport outside *Kennedy* Building at *15.30* (*or 3.30*) ☑
6 Second *coach* at *17.15* (or *5.15*). Delegates to arrive five minutes before departure.
7 Drs Schapsinger, Garbeldi and Surinander: collect *reprints* from conference *desk.*
8 Dr Goldman (*Chicago* Institute) 6th Annual Convention of *P.E.S.*, in *Hawaii*, in *October 1986.* Interested parties leave *name* at conference *desk.* ☑

Practice

A

1 *If* I *could* have your *attention* for a moment please.
2 I *would like* to *see* you return them to the session chairpeople. I'd *like* to *ask* you all to be there, ready for the buses . . .
3 We're moving the final discussion to Room 201. *That's* Room 201. Which means that the domestic shelter session will be changed from Room 201 to Room 304. *That's* the domestic shelter session in Room 304.
4 Thank you.
5 Ladies and gentlemen.

Note

There are other ways of making polite requests than those used by this speaker: *I wonder if I could, Could I possibly, Might I, May I,* etc.

B

1 Now, *first of all,* I'd like to mention
2 *Now,* I have a *notice here*
3 *Turning now* to your discussion records
4 *Regarding* coaches to the airport
5 I have *particular messages* for Dr Schapsinger
6 *Finally,* I have a reminder

Speaking

Ladies and gentlemen, *if I could have your attention for a moment, please.* We're arriving at the Alhambra now, and there are a few important things I need to say.
First of all, please remove all valuables from the coach, because we can't guarantee their safety. *That's* all cameras, bags of value, etc. *Thank you. Now,* it would be a good idea to make a note of the number on the front of the coach, 361, so that you can recognize it in the coach park.
Turning to the tour, *I'd like to ask you all to* stay with your own party and guide. Please don't wander off as the site's very large and you can get lost easily. So please keep with your group. *Thank you.*
Regarding photographs – these can only be taken at certain points on the site, so please obey your guide's instructions. *That's* photographs – please watch the restrictions.
Finally, ladies and gentlemen, the coach will leave the coach park at 18.15 – *that's* 6.15 – so please be on time. Have an enjoyable tour. *Thank you.*

2 An Aussie at Eton

Eton, founded in 1440, is probably the best known of Britain's private schools, which cater for about 3% of the population. Eton is a boarding school for boys only, and in the recording various of its idiosyncratic traditions and activities are discussed. The most difficult aspect of the interview is the speaker's ironical attitude to his subject. Students should read carefully the ringed information in the article and listen to check specific facts.
Accent: RP; Australian

Tapescript

Interviewer But first the third in our series of interviews with those people who so influence our children – teachers. Today we move from state school teachers to that most exclusive of private schools, Eton College. And we have Charles Mason here with us. Hello, Charles.
Mason Hello there.
Interviewer Now. You've been teaching at Eton for two terms, I think, and you're an Australian. Erm, what were your first impressions when you started at this very, very British school?
Mason Well, I found one or two things there rather difficult to come to terms with. It's a school that has er, all sorts of eccentric things that, er . . .
Interviewer Uhuh.
Mason . . . relating to the language that the boys use, the er, clothes that they wear, the way that they behave.
Interviewer Could you tell me some of those?
Mason Well, you know they have to wear this ridiculous tail-coat.
Interviewer Uhuh.
Mason And they wear funny collars, er, stick-up collars they call them. Anyone else would call them wing collars.
Interviewer Uhuh.
Mason They wear white bow ties.
Interviewer Uhuh.
Mason They wear these stripy trousers which are, apart from anything else, I'm told, incredibly hot and uncomfortable to wear.
Interviewer And what do you wear, as teachers?
Mason Oh, I just wear perfectly normal clothes. I've got to wear, er, striped trousers as well and a black jacket . . .
Interviewer Uhuh.
Mason . . . and a wing collar and a white bow tie.
Interviewer Uhuh.
Mason And I've got to wear a gown every time that I walk into a classroom . . .
Interviewer All the time?
Mason Yep . . .
Interviewer Uhuh.
Mason Every time I walk into a classroom, I've got to wear a gown.
Interviewer Is it true that there's a secret language at Eton?
Mason Well, it's not only a secret language. I mean, a boy will come up to you and say, 'Sir, I've just seen, er seen, old Twisleton-Wykeham-Fiennes socking erm, Smythens,' and you wonder what on earth's . . .

Interviewer Mm.
Mason . . . been going on. All it means is he's been giving him something to eat. And they have other sort of strange, eccentric terms as well. 'Mobbing', for example. Mobbing just means er, gathering round and listening to somebody talking.
Interviewer But you . . .
Mason Well . . .
Interviewer Yes, sorry. Go on.
Mason Well. They have all sorts of secret signs as well. Well, they're not secret they're . . . they're damn blatant.
Interviewer Uhuh.
Mason For example, capping. Capping's, er, every time a boy walks past a master he's got to raise one finger, like that. Well, the first time I saw this I thought . . .
Interviewer It was a rude gesture.
Mason I thought it was a rude gesture. Absolutely.
Interviewer Yes.
Mason But no, it goes back to the days when the boys wore top hats . . .
Interviewer Uhuh.
Mason . . . and every time a master walked past, he raised his top hat to the master.
Interviewer But how does this strike you? I mean, you come from a much more egalitarian society in Australia. Don't you find this weird, or even offensive?
Mason I don't find it offensive. I just find it really weird and it's, it's mildly entertaining for a couple of . . .
Interviewer Mm.
Mason . . . weeks. Novelty wears off after a while and, er . . .
Interviewer Mm.
Mason . . . I've lost interest now in raising my finger to the two or three boys who walk past me in the street.
Interviewer Uhuh. What do you think it does offer that other schools perhaps can't?
Mason It offers, apart from the sort of education that I suppose you'd expect from a place with the qualified staff they've got and the, er . . .
Interviewer Mm.
Mason . . . amount of facilities they can afford. If you've got parents paying virtually six thousand pounds a year . . .
Interviewer Mm.
Mason . . . you're going to be able to afford a fairly decent set of equipment. But it, er, offers a chance for your children to learn eccentric games as well like, er, the wall game, field game, games that can't be played in any other part of the world.
Interviewer So it doesn't fit you, necessarily, particularly well for the real world outside?
Mason I doubt that it fits you any better than any school . . .
Interviewer Mm. So you wouldn't . . .
Mason . . . does.
Interviewer . . . recommend that I put my son down for Eton?
Mason Well, you know I can't answer a question like that.
Interviewer Well, thank you very much. That was extremely interesting.
Mason Thank you.
Interviewer Next week we'll be interviewing a teacher from an inner-city . . .

Language items

Twisleton-Wykeham-Fiennes: boys in public schools are usually addressed by their family names. The interviewee purposely chooses an authentic but ludicrous triple-barrelled family name for one of the pupils.
socking: hitting (slang)
put my son down for Eton: parents who wish to send their son to Eton must put his name on a waiting list at birth, or even before

Note

The terminology used to distinguish various educational institutions in Britain is often confusing. *State* or *maintained* schools: schools financed by central and local government. *Private* schools: schools which are not government-financed and which charge fees, also known as *independent* schools. The oldest and best known of these are called *public* schools, because they were originally financed by public subscription. Eton is a public school.

Listening

A
1 F **2** F **3** T **4** N **5** T
6 T **7** F **8** N **9** F **10** F

B
1c 2c 3d

Practice

A

first impressions	eccentric terms
ridiculous tailcoat	blatant signs
funny collars	rude gesture
stripy trousers	egalitarian society
normal clothes	qualified staff
secret language	decent (set of) equipment

B
Although almost any combination of adjectives and nouns is possible when the language is being

used creatively, students should concern themselves with developing a feeling for standard uses, so that they can use them, and recognize departures from them. The table here indicates the most likely combination of the listed adjectives and nouns.

	terms	trousers	gesture	signs	tailcoat	clothes	collars	staff	impressions	equipment	language	society
first			√	√					√		√	
ridiculous	√	√	√	√	√	√	√	√	√	√	√	√
funny	√	√	√	√	√	√	√	√	√	√	√	√
stripy		√			√	√	√					
normal	√	√	√	√	√	√	√	√	√	√	√	√
secret	√		√	√					√		√	√
eccentric	√	√	√	√	√	√	√	√	√	√	√	√
blatant	√		√	√							√	
rude	√	√	√	√		√		√	√	√	√	√
egalitarian	√					√		√			√	√
qualified	√							√				
decent	√	√	√	√	√	√	√	√	√	√	√	√

3 While you were out

Patrick Lechlade is a professional photographer. The first and the third messages are related to his work and therefore the style is fairly formal. The second and fourth calls are personal, and are much more informal. Listeners should extract the message and try to ignore the inessential chatter. Accent: RP; American; London; advanced RP

Tapescript

1

Erm, my name is Antonia North. I'm secretary to Jenny Pargeter, Social Editor of *Tutler*, and she's asked me to ring you to see if you can do a photographic feature on erm, a VIP. I, I, I'm afraid I can't tell you who it is over the phone. Erm, Mrs Pargeter would like to see you at the beginning of next week because she is going away, and she suggested that you might like to have lunch at Brown's. I hope that's all right. Thank you.

2

Hey, er, Patrick. Hi there. It's Sam Schoenberg. You remember me? You know, from Harvard Graduate School? Right. You got it. Now listen. I've just come into London. Now, I'm gonna be staying – I – Actually, I, I should be staying at the Hilton but I, I, I'm not. We won't go into that. Listen, I'm at a couple of friends' er, who live in Hampstead. Hampstead. I'll tell you the number. It's 435-7175. You got that? OK. Now, listen. Their names are Joan and Christopher Orton. Hey, Patrick, now I'm in town for a few days. I'm promoting my new book. You know, 'Staying Young – Cosmetic Surgery in the 80s'. Well, listen. You, er, gotta get in touch with me. I want to see you, it's been a long time and er, call my friends up. Tell them you're around, what time you can see me and er, we'll get together, all right? OK, listen, we'll see you, Patrick.

3

Oh, erm . . . yeah. Erm, this is er, Wayne Jones here from Photomart Ltd. Erm, I was asked by, er, Brian Tidmarsh, he's my boss you know, to er, ring you up and tell you that those colour filters that you ordered erm . . . well, they're unavailable. So, er, do you want to, replace another order for another type of filter, or do you wanna cancel the order altogether? Er, yeah, that's the end of the message.

4

Or, er, hello Patrick, old thing. It's, it's Marty, Marty Hunt. Erm, from the old days, if you remember. We were at school together. Er, we met actually, er, last Christmas at Samantha's party. Erm . . . er, but the point is erm, I wonder, could you, could you help me out? Erm . . . er, you see, I er, I've been on holiday recently in Crete, the old Ayios Nikolaos and I took my box Brownie er, and I've got some rather interesting pictures and erm, er, well, some rather smashing Swedish birds at a barbecue. Yes. Er, used my flash. More ways than one! Well, but erm, the point is I, I don't actually want them to be developed at my local chemist. I think it might, might raise his hair. So I wonder, could I pop along to your studio and, and use your, your facilities? Er, I mean, they're, they're nothing, you know, there's nothing too awful about them at all. I mean, nothing, nothing that er, would surprise you. I mean, after all, all those tyre calendars you took. All those smashing birds in Africa. I don't know, some people have all the luck. Erm, anyway, that, that is the situation so erm . . . er, if you could sort of, er, phone me back er, or rather I'll phone you. Er, cheerio.

Language items

a VIP: a very important person (V-I-P)
gonna be: going to be
gotta: got to
wanna: want to
replace another order: place another order (the speaker makes a slip)
box Brownie: an old-fashioned kind of camera
smashing: remarkably fine or attractive (colloquial)
birds: women (colloquial and derogatory)
raise his hair: surprise or shock him

Listening

A

3 ☑ **5** ☑ **6** ☑ **7** ☑

B

2 Mr Sam Schoenberg telephoned, wants to see you, please ring.
Phone no: 435-7175
Message: in *London* few days, staying with *Ortons*.
3 Mr Wayne Jones of Photomart Ltd telephoned.
Message: *colour filters* not available. *Cancel* or change order?
4 Mr Marty Hunt (old school friend) telephoned, will ring again.
Message: wants to *borrow your facilities* (or *dark room*).

Practice

A

1 *My name is* Antonia North.
3 *It's* Sam Schoenberg.
3 *This is* Wayne Jones.

Note

I am Antonia North is not acceptable in this context (the telephone).

B

1 She's *asked* me *to ring* you –
2 *to* see *if* you can do a photographic feature on a VIP.
3 Mrs Pargeter *would* like *to see* you at the beginning of next week *because* she's going away.
4 She suggested *that* you *might like* to have lunch at Brown's.

Notes

1 A direct question with 'can' ('Can he do a photographic feature?'), becomes 'could/if' ('. . . to see if you can/could do a photographic feature').
2 The verb 'to suggest' is not followed by the same syntactic pattern as 'to ask' and 'to tell':

she suggested (that) he { ring / rang / might ring / might like to ring }

Speaking

Antonia Jenny Pargeter's office. Antonia North speaking.
Jonathan Oh hello. This is Jonathan Bell, Patrick Lechlade's P.A. Mr Lechlade asked me to ring to confirm that he can do your photo feature provided it's this month.
Antonia Oh good. Yes, it is this month. Now, Mrs Pargeter would like to have lunch with Mr Lechlade on Monday, to fix the details. Would that be convenient?
Jonathan Well, that'd be possible, but Mr Lechlade would prefer Tuesday, if that suits you.
Antonia Yes, fine. 12.30 at Brown's?
Jonathan Mmm. Well, actually, Mr Lechlade's not very keen on Brown's. In fact, he suggested that they might like to meet at Langham's.
Antonia Langham's? Okay, I suppose that'll be all right. 12.30 at Langham's on Tuesday then.
Jonathan Well, Mr Lechlade might find 12.30 a bit on the early side – he's got rather a tight schedule on Tuesday morning. Could we make it 1.30?
Antonia Let me see . . . No, I'm afraid Mrs Pargeter's got a meeting at 2.30 so it would have to be earlier. What about 12.45?
Jonathan One o'clock?
Antonia Okay, let's make it one o'clock then. So it's one o'clock, Tuesday, at Langham's. I'll book a table.
Jonathan Thank you very much.
Antonia Thank you. Goodbye.
Jonathan Goodbye.

4 A woman's place

Much of the meaning and interest in this recording comes from *how* something is said even more than *what* is said. Students should therefore pay careful attention to stress and intonation when attempting the exercises.
Accent: RP; RP

Tapescript

Anne Harry?
Harry Hmm.
Anne Have you seen this ad?
Harry No, what? What is it?
Anne Well, look. It says, 'If you want a merry Christmas, treat your wife to a Superchef, now.'
Harry Ah, yes. Mm, mm it would be quite useful, wouldn't it?
Anne Well, of course it would be useful, dear. But that's not what I'm talking about. Look. Look at this woman.
Harry Yes, well. What about her?
Anne Well. It says, 'If you want a merry Christmas, *treat* your wife to a Superchef now.'
Harry Are you trying to tell me something, darling? I mean, do you . . .
Anne Well, I . . .
Harry . . . want a Superchef?
Anne No, of course I don't. What I'm trying to tell you is, that it's not a present. I mean it, it, it's a kitchen aid. A present should be something personal. There are, there are ads now which suggest that *women* should give *men* diamond tie pins and gold jewellery, not power tools and paint brushes.
Harry Yes. Well, you always give me socks, don't you?
Anne You're, you're not . . .
Harry I've a drawer full of socks. Plaid socks, plain socks, green socks . . .
Anne All right, dear, all right, dear. I'm not suggesting that you give me tights. All I'm saying is, that there is no question of this woman having a merry Christmas at all because she's going to be far too busy, slaving away in the kitchen . . .
Harry No.
Anne . . . with her Christmas present.
Harry Just a minute. I know what you're on about. And it's one of your, sort of, Women's Lib things. No. Look. The whole point about this, is she's *not* going to be slaving away, is she? She's going to switch this on and it's going to do all these wonderful things and mix things and all this sort of thing.
Anne Yes, I know. But she's . . .
Harry While she's enjoying it, you know. Wearing her new frock or whatever it is . . .
Anne Harry. Harry.
Harry Her luxury present that she's got . . .
Anne She's got to . . .
Harry . . . and putting on her new perfume and . . .
Anne Listen. She's got to be in the kitchen looking after the machine. It doesn't do it by itself. So. She is going to be slaving away, as I say, with this marvellous kitchen aid – to give her husband, not to mention the whole family, a happy Christmas. It's preposterous . . .
Harry Well, I don't see why she shouldn't be, you know.
Anne . . . it's preposterous.
Harry I don't see why she shouldn't be. I mean, my mother slaved away, and there were five of us . . .
Anne Oh, there's no use talking to you.

Language items

Superchef: a make of food processor
ad(s): advertisement(s) (abbreviation)
plaid: tartan cloth woven of coloured stripes
Women's Lib: Women's Liberation (Movement)
slaving away: working very hard, like a slave
preposterous: totally unreasonable

Listening

A
1 c **2** c **3** b **4** a **5** a
6 c **7** c **8** b **9** b **10** b

Practice

A
1 b
2 c
3 b
4 a
5 No. His voice rises at the end of the sentence, indicating that he has more to add to the list.
6 a

B
These answers are open to discussion, as determining mood depends, to a certain extent, on personal interpretation. The answers given below are intended as a guide only.
1 c **2** b **3** c **4** e
5 c **6** a **7** b **8** d

5 Hard sell

This recording consists of two very short commercial advertisements from the radio. The first requires intensive listening, the second listening for information.
Accent: American; American

Tapescript

1

Female Makeway shopping is quality at low prices, on the kind of things you and I need every week.

Male And this week you'll find quality brands like new richer Aladdin Liquid to last even longer, new improved Wave Automatic to wash even whiter, new April-fresh Countrycare to caress even closer.

Female So come Makeway shopping for quality at low prices.

2

Male From the Hot Bananas to the Salzburg Boys' Choir, from Opera '85 to Nellie and the Melbas, there's a superb line-up of entertainment planned for the fall season at the Hepburn Theater. There's something for everyone from country music to award-winning drama. Booking starts on August (the) 13th. For details, call the Hepburn box office on 994-1528.

Language items

Makeway: name of a supermarket
brand: a particular make (of goods)
caress: touch lovingly, kiss (used here to suggest softness)
fall: autumn (American English)

Listening

A

1 Aladdin Liquid, Wave Automatic, Countrycare
2 b
3 b
4 a
5 c

B

These are just some of the events planned for the *fall* season

The *Salzburg Boys'* Choir

The *Hot* Bananas
Nellie and the Melbas
Opera *'85*
Entertainment for *everyone*
Booking starts *August 13th*
Ring the Hepburn box office now on *994-1528*

Practice

A

1 quality
2 low
3 prices
4 week
5 even
6 new
7 (Makeway shopping)

B

Sparkle floor polish to make your floor even shinier . . .
Zing toothpaste to leave your teeth even whiter, your breath even fresher . . .
New improved *Waistline tropical fruit drink,* to taste even better, help you lose weight even faster . . .
Summer Days air freshener to smell even sweeter, last even longer . . .

Note

The recording demonstrates three techniques popularly used by advertisers: alliteration (beginning words with the same letter) – *Aladdin Liquid to last even longer*
repetition – *quality, even, low prices*
contrast – *from The Hot Bananas to the Salzburg Boys' Choir*

C

For the purposes of accuracy, only the accented syllable of the stressed words has been underlined.

Makeway shopping is quality at low prices on the kind of things you and I need every week . . . So come Makeway shopping for quality at low prices.

Speaking

Colin's crazy clearance sale starts on Friday, (the) 27th (of) July. There are massive price reductions on furniture, carpets and curtain fabrics. You'd have to be out of your mind to miss it. Colin's crazy clearance sale starting Friday, (the) 27th (of) July, at Colin's, in the Brunel Plaza, Swindon.

6 What's my line?

These are six short extracts of people interviewed while at work. Students should listen for clues to identify each job.
Accent: Irish; RP; Scottish; Northern; RP; Northern

Tapescript

1 Well now Mrs Jenkins. Er, I'm afraid it is too late. Yes, she, she will have to be put down. But, er, yes, she's had a good innings now hasn't she? Oh, she's, er, what is she, fifteen? Yeah. You see, in cases like this there's nothing we can do, really. I mean, and she, she's blind and well, she would only be suffering, no matter what we did. So, it would be for the best, believe me.

2 That's great, er, Wendy. Erm, just hang on a second. Er, colour . . . right. Erm, tell you what, just move slightly to the right. No, other way, other way. That . . . bit less . . . good! Hold it there, hold it there. Right. Er, stay still. Just lick your lips a second. That's good. OK. Hold it. And . . . great. Good. And again. OK just turn slightly towards me, slightly, other way, other way. Good. Hold it . . .

3 Now just stay – sit there and relax. That's right. Now let me have a look. Open. That's fine. Och, no. This is quite easy. Just a wee drop of cement. That's all you need.

4 Well, when I saw the job in the paper, it said 'Go out and meet people!' you know. So, I thought, 'Well that'll be the job for me, really.' So I went out and I had a little look, and now I've got the job and I do like meeting people. But you're outdoors all day. You know, when the rain comes and it's downing it, you don't half get sore feet. People expect me to be fat and horrible and old and pokey and I'm not like that at all really. I mean, I'm – I understand their problems, you know. They come up to me and they say, 'Well, there's double yellow lines everywhere.' 'Well,' I say, 'I know it's difficult, I mean, what with the traffic jams and all that,' and I say, 'Well, I'll give you five minutes, just five minutes, love, and then you'll have to be off and on your way, all right?' And some of them think I'm a little Hitler, but I'm not.

5 **Interviewer** Can you tell us how you actually feel as you wait?

Actor Well, er, it's 7.59. The curtain goes up in one minute. I'm standing in the wings, sort of tense but er, excited. I wonder what kind of house it is, you know, how big it is. They seem to be pretty good tonight. Every evening there's a different atmosphere in the house . . .

6 **Interviewer** What sort of person do you have to be to do this sort of job ?

Fire-fighter Well, you gotta be right fit. I mean, look at them blokes over there. Look at them. I mean look at muscles on them there, cleaning that thing. And, er, well, you gotta be all right with heights. You're not going to be afraid of that. And er, you gotta do shift work, 'cos we're on, er, 365 days a year, you see. So there's that to take into account, 'cos you get your busy times and you get your slack times. And when it's a bit slack, you play cards or sit around, you know, having a laugh with the lads or whatever. Sometimes you get a hoax. Bloody daft, i'n't it? Hoax! You go out there and nobody wants to know, you know. They say, 'What you come here for?' and we say, 'Well, you know, we had a, we had a special call come through . . .'

Language items

to put down: to kill (animals) humanely
a good innings: lived a long time (cricketing term)
och: oh (Scottish)
wee: small (Scottish)
cement: (dental) cement to fill teeth
you don't half get sore feet: you get very sore feet (colloquial)
pokey: interfering (local corruption of 'to poke one's nose into something')
double yellow lines: lines painted along the side of the road to indicate a no-parking area
love: a colloquial form of address denoting friendliness; it carries no emotional overtones
little Hitler: a term to describe a person who is thought to be dictatorial
wings: unseen area to either side of a theatre stage
gotta: got to
right fit: very fit (Yorkshire dialect)
blokes: men (colloquial)
look at muscles: look at the muscles (Yorkshire)
shift work: work situation in which one group of workers starts as another group finishes, so that all twenty-four hours of the day can be covered
slack times: times when there is little work to be done
hoax: trick intended to deceive
daft: silly (colloquial)
i'n't it?: isn't it? (Yorkshire)
What you come here for?: What have you come here for? (Yorkshire)

Listening

1 c **2** h **3** g **4** f **5** d **6** j

Practice

A

1 their, you

2 *You don't half get sore feet* – she must do a lot of walking.

People expect me to be fat and horrible and old and pokey – the public does not have a pleasant image of people who do her job, so it is not an occupation where people are pleased to see her.

I understand their problems – but she does not say what kind of problems these are.

I know it's difficult – but she does not say what is difficult.

3 traffic jams

B

You only have to look at me to realize my problem. People call me Fatso, but I can't help it because I've got to check that the flavour's right. Sometimes I'm rushed off my feet – everyone wants everything at the same time. It can get very hot and steamy and the hours are long, but I like my work because it's creative, and I get congratulated on it by satisfied customers. Even so, my wife teases me for doing what she calls 'women's work'.

7 Plain sailing

The sailing instructor's delivery is informal and jocular, but he is very much in control. He is authoritative without being authoritarian. Students should familiarize themselves with the sketch map and the nautical terms relevant to the task before attempting to complete it.
Accent: West Country

Tapescript

Instructor Right. I think everyone's here now. Now, settle down and concentrate. You'll need a lot of energy today, so I hope you had a good breakfast. Now, er, you've all got a sketch map of the estuary. (Oh, erm, I haven't got one.) Oh, sorry, here you are Jane. Late as usual. Right. We'll leave at nine a.m. prompt. We want to catch the ebb tide. Now, don't forget your life-jackets and of course thick sweater and anorak. It'll be cold as you get near the open sea. OK, ready to mark in the course? Right. Now you'll start from between the two launches – you see I've drawn them in at the bottom of the map there. Now, tack upwind, down river heading towards the wood on the east shore. Round the buoy, leaving it to port and head towards the marina. Er, no, Sarah, to port. Right. Now make sure as you go round the buoy, near the jetty, not to hit any of the moored boats. Remember Wednesday, John? There's a tricky manoeuvre coming now. Leaving that buoy to starboard, head back to the wood and round south of the buoy towards the bridge and back on a figure of eight course rounding the second buoy again. (Oh no!) All right, all right, I'll go through that again. This is where we'll be testing you on all points of sailing. You leave the buoy to starboard. Aim for the wood, go to the south of the buoy. Yes, yes, that's right, John. The one on the way to the bridge, and come back on a figure of eight course, going round the second buoy, the one near the jetty, again. OK? Now you all got that? (Yes. Think so. Yes.) Now do remember that a boat on a starboard tack has right of way, so if someone shouts 'starboard' get out of the way, and fast! Now, head towards the wreck. Now you'll have marked that. Be careful, or you might end up one yourself . . . (Like me the other day.) Fortunately, it'll be an off-shore wind at that point, so you should have no trouble. Keep close to the buoy anyway. Now, once clear of the wreck, aim for the headland on the east side of the estuary, keeping clear of the rocks, and rounding the next buoy. Head across to the cliffs on the west side, keeping outside the two buoys at the base of the cliffs, but it is safe to go inshore of the moored barge, you'll see that's marked. Right, from there you tack upwind, leaving the island to port. Now you'll be coming into open sea, so the water'll be choppy so please be careful. Remember if you do capsize the rescue launch'll be at hand. And, Alan, no swimming to shore. The golden rule is stay with your boat. Now once past the island, head to the port side of the lighthouse. Round it completely in a clockwise direction. Er, no Peter, in a clockwise direction. (That's this way round.) This'll mean a gybe. So, Anne, if you don't want another bruise on the top of your head, remember to duck as the boom goes across. (Keep your woolly hat on.) Right, from here you head due west to the bay in the cliffs just past the castle. And that's where you'll be able to relax. We're going to have a barbecue. Oh, er, by the way, don't forget to bring your swimming things. Lower the mainsail and come in just on the jib.

Er, although we'll be er, timing you, don't think of it as a race. The most important thing is to follow the course I've given you. And don't worry if you're at the end of the fleet. I promise you there'll still be plenty to eat – and drink. Right, have a great sail. See you at lunchtime. (Right . . .)

Language items

ebb tide: the flow of sea (tide) back from land to sea
life-jackets: vests made of buoyant material to support body in water
anorak: waterproof jacket with hood attached
tack upwind: move upwind by sailing in a zig-zag fashion with the wind first on one side, then on the other
heading towards: going in the direction of
port: left (sailing term)
marina: harbour for pleasure boats
starboard: right (sailing term)
on a starboard tack: with the wind on the starboard side
choppy: rough (of the sea)
gybe: to cause the boom to swing from one side of the boat to the other when the wind is behind it
to duck: to move quickly down to avoid being hit (or seen)
boom: movable horizontal pole to which bottom of sail is attached
jib: a triangular sail, smaller than the mainsail
fleet: a number of boats or ships all moving in the same direction

Note

Definitions of the sailing terms have been given for the sake of clarity and for teachers' reference. It is not necessary to understand them all in order to complete the exercises.

Listening

See map below.

Practice

A

1 estuary **2** tide **3** launch **4** buoy **5** jetty
6 wreck **7** barge **8** lighthouse

B

1 (*Now*) *don't forget* your life-jackets
2 *Make sure* as you go round the buoy
3 (*Now*) *do remember* that a boat on a starboard tack has right of way
4 *Be careful,* or you might end up one yourself

C

1 *Head* back to the wood
2 *Aim* for the wood

Speaking

We'll meet at the car park at ten o'clock. Don't forget to wear strong shoes, and it might rain, so remember to bring an anorak. Now, I'll tell you your route. Come out of the car park and turn right. A few metres along the road you'll see a farm gate on your left. Go through it but don't forget to shut it securely. Cross the field aiming for the stile opposite and make sure you keep to the path. Be careful not to tread on any of the corn growing there, etc . . .

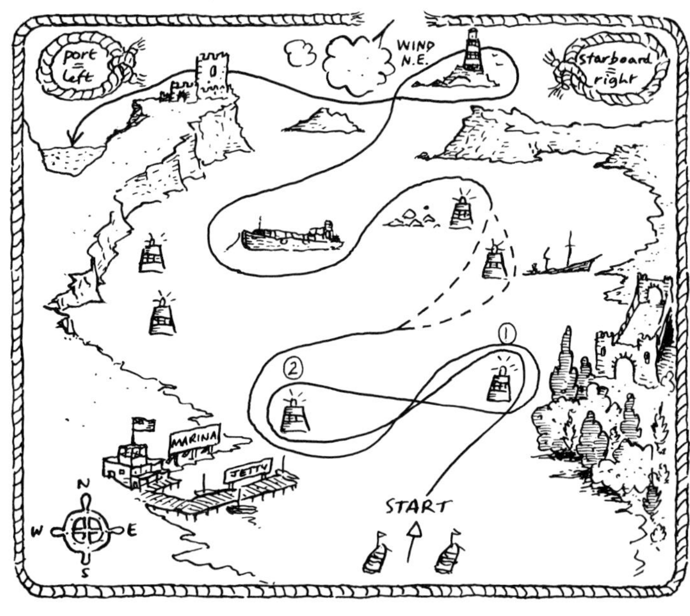

8 Till death us do part

The recording begins in the middle of an informal conversation between acquaintances, none of whom is a native speaker. The societies talked about are Hindu India, where the traditional arranged marriages continue in modified form, Christian Protestant Denmark, where marriage had become outdated but is now gaining in popularity again, and Christian Catholic Brazil, where the State now accepts, but does not encourage, divorce. Listeners may need to familiarize themselves with the accent before attempting the whole task.
Accent: Indian; Danish; Brazilian

Tapescript

Usha Yeah, most of the Indian marriages work out very well I think, although they are arranged. Yes.
Hanne But Usha didn't say yes to the first one, did you?
Usha No. Well, as I said, we do have, erm, the choice whether we would like to get married or not, so we can say yes or no. And I did say no to two people.
Hanne Is it a nice, big fancy wedding? How was yours?
Usha Yes. Most of Indian marriages are elaborate marriages and er, my marriage went on for three days and we had a lot of guests as well.
Hanne How many people were there?
Usha Well, in my marriage, er, we had about three thousand, two thousand guests.
Hanne Ai, ai! Well, it doesn't matter if it's two or three with that number.
Usha Yes.
Hanne Do you have to feed them or are they just hanging around with . . .
Usha Yes. The interesting thing about it is in Indian marriages even the very poor man has about a hundred guests.
Hanne Mm.
Usha And it depends on the status in the society, his status in the society.
Hanne Big families, fine families . . .
Usha Yes, big families.
Hanne . . . lots of food . . .
Usha Yes . . .
Hanne . . . little families, not so much.
Usha Yes, that's right. Yes.
Hanne How was your . . . are you married?
Lea No, I'm divorced.
Hanne Oh, are you?
Lea Yeah, yeah.
Hanne So people *can* get a divorce in Brazil?
Lea Oh, yes. We can. Well, since 1980.
Hanne Uhuh.
Lea Yes, because, er, before it was not allowed. But er, even so, we can get married just twice in Brazil, you know. A third time is not allowed.
Hanne Oh!
Lea Yeah.
Hanne So you already, er lost half your . . .
Lea Yes. It's my last chance now.
Hanne Well . . .
Usha How about the marriages in Scandinavia, Hanne?
Hanne Well, people don't make much of an ado about it. Most people er, just move in together, they don't even bother to get a licence, especially some years ago. That has caused lots of er, legal confusion though . . .
Lea Mm.
Hanne . . . because when they split up you don't know whose is what and why and . . . no. And so now they get married again. They tend to get married more often. But it's just a simple church wedding or a visit to the registrar's office.
Lea Oh with . . .
Hanne Hmm. How about in your country?
Lea Well, it's still a strong institution in our society, you know. But it depends. It concerns the upper and middle classes, because among the poor people they don't get married at all. They just live together and separate and that's all.
Hanne And you had a fancy wedding?
Lea Oh no, no, mine was simple. I didn't want . . .
Hanne And is it the bride's family who does all that?
Lea Oh yes, yes, yes. Well, nowadays they share the expenses, but, you know, the tradition is that the bride do this.
Hanne Oh.
Usha Very interesting. It seems very different from what we have in India.
Hanne Yeah. Who, who . . .
Lea Who pays?
Usha The bride's parents pay . . .
Hanne Mm.
Usha . . . they meet all the expenses.
Hanne Yeah . . .
Lea Ah, yeah.
Hanne . . . Still nowadays?
Usha Yes. Yes, very much.
Hanne In Denmark, it's usually the, the bride or the bridegroom who have to pay.
Usha Yes.
Hanne The parents won't have anything to do with it.
Usha Yes. I was talking of divorce – although it is legalized in India, it is very uncommon that we have any divorces at all. And it's very interesting

to know that as most of the Indian marriages are arranged marriages, we have very few divorces.
Hanne Oh, I don't believe it . . . !

Language items

(Well, it doesn't matter if it's two or three with that number.) Yes: Usha is agreeing with Hanne, so her response should be 'No' (. . . it doesn't matter)
a licence: a marriage licence.
registrar's office (also *registry office*): place where records of births, marriages and deaths are kept and couples can get a marriage licence
the bride do this: the bride does this

Listening

India: Most marriages *arranged*, but girl can *refuse*. Weddings v. *elaborate*; size depends on groom's *status* in society. Even v. poor man has *100* guests. Bride's parents meet all wedding *expenses*. Divorce *legal* but v. *rare*.
Brazil: Marriage still a strong *institution* among middle and upper classes. Poor people just *live together* and then *separate*. Nowadays, wedding expenses *shared*. Traditionally, *bride's* parents responsible. Divorce possible since *1980*, but people only allowed to re-marry *once*.
Denmark: Until recently, most people just *lived together*, and didn't bother to *get married*. This presented legal problems when couple *separated*, so now marriage becoming more *popular* again. Ceremony – simple *church* wedding or *registrar's* office. Usually paid for by *bride* and/or *bridegroom*.

Practice

A

1 to put *together*
2 to work *out*
3 to go *on*
4 to hang *around*
5 to depend *on*
6 to move *in together*
7 to split *up*
8 to live *together*

B

Miss Sharon Griffiths, of School Road, Leafield, was *married* to Mr Colin Weeks of London at St Mary's *Church*, Leafield. The *bride's* parents are Mr and Mrs John Griffiths, of Leafield, and the *bridegroom* is the son of Mr Daniel Weeks and the late Mrs Weeks.

The *best man* was Mr Julian Weeks, and the *bride* was attended by *bridesmaids* Tracey Weeks and Julie Hicks. The *ceremony* was conducted by Rev David Wise and the *reception* was held at Leafield Village Hall. The newlyweds are spending their *honeymoon* in the Canary Islands.

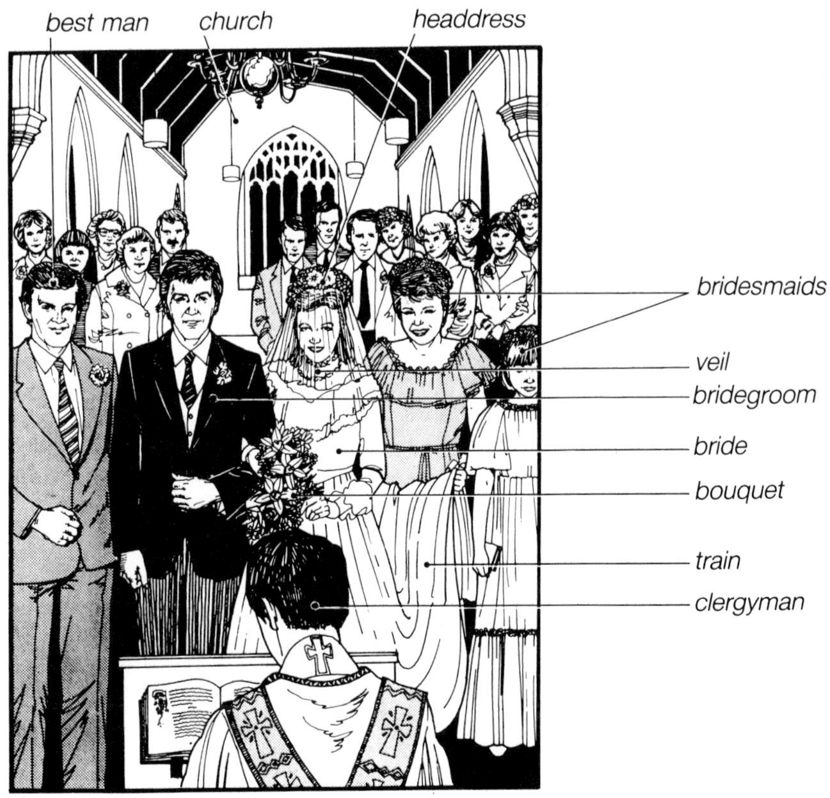

9 Another country

This is an informal interview. Listeners may need to familiarize themselves with the accent before attempting the whole task.
Accent: RP; Caribbean

Tapescript

Interviewer Well, Berry, everybody knows you at the college. Erm, and who, what, what do you actually do?
Berry I'm a caretaker at the college. And I work there for over four years.
Interviewer Mm.
Berry And I looking after the college. Open the doors . . .
Interviewer Mm.
Berry . . . and do a bit of security work. Make sure that everybody's happy, looking after the admin staff and also the lecturer.
Interviewer Mm. Mm. So you work shifts, do you? Or what?
Berry Yes, we work shifts. I work from five to two, and from two to ten.
Interviewer Mm.
Berry So, it's, it's not a bad number.
Interviewer And when did you, when did you first come to England?
Berry In 1960 from the West Indies.
Interviewer Whereabouts in the West Indies?
Berry St Vincent.
Interviewer Uhuh. And how did you find it, coming to England?
Berry Well, at first it was not all that nice but by living here . . .
Interviewer It must have been cold.
Berry Yeah. It was rather cold, I was freezing.
Interviewer Mm.
Berry But by living here for so long, you know, I get to like the place and adapt myself . . .
Interviewer Mm.
Berry . . . to the people that are in it.
Interviewer Mm. And why did you come to Oxford?
Berry Well, Oxford. I have some relative was living in Oxford when they first came to England so . . .
Interviewer Mm.
Berry . . . by writing home and telling my parents well Oxford was nice, so I decide to come and join them.
Interviewer So what did, what did you do when you first came then?
Berry Well . . .
Interviewer Did you have a job to come to?
Berry Well, no, I didn't. But they were working so they tried to get me in where they were.
Interviewer Mm. And where did . . . where, where was your first job?
Berry Well, the first one I start was at the bakery. At the Co-op bakery in Botley Road, and I work there for a little over eleven and a half years.
Interviewer And why did you leave there?
Berry Well, they closed the place down. They made, made me redundant.
Interviewer Mm.
Berry So I have to leave . . .
Interviewer Mm.
Berry . . . look for another job which I get one at Morris's.
Interviewer Morris's? What's . . .
Berry Yes. That's British Leyland . . .
Interviewer Ah, yeah.
Berry . . . in Cowley. And then I work there for over eight, eight and a half years. And after leaving there, I get a job at the college.
Interviewer Mm.
Berry Which is quite near to me. We only live . . .
Interviewer Oh, you live just round the corner . . .
Berry Yes.
Interviewer . . . don't you?
Berry Uhuh.
Berry And then, well . . . meeting these nice people, I decide to stick it there.
Interviewer Oh yes. I heard, I heard that you sell, I hear that you sell cosmetics there too. That's rather unusual, isn't it?
Berry Yes. My wife asked me to do it, you know, say well, I have a luck with the girls, a lot of charm . . . so, so I decide to sell it for her. And I, I do very well.
Interviewer So how do you actually sell it to them? Do you . . .
Berry Well, I just go and ask them if they like this . . .
Interviewer Mm.
Berry . . . and they say, 'Yes, I like it.' So they just buy it from me and then I keep taking more to them.
Interviewer So you don't actually do any demonstrations, or anything like that?
Berry No, not a lot, not a lot . . . I'd like to, but not a lot. I have a lot of friends and they say, 'Berry, could you bring my Avon book for me to see what you have?' and so on, which I do. So I try to sell what I could sell for my wife, and so on, you know.
Interviewer Yeah.
Berry It's not a bad . . .
Interviewer So how long have you been doing that then?
Berry Well, for a few years now . . .
Interviewer Mm.

Berry . . . I've been doing it for.
Interviewer So really, you're, you're helping her to sell?
Berry Yes. I helping her to sell.
Interviewer Mm.

Language items

*I work there for over four years**: I worked there for over four years
*I looking after the college**: I look after the college
admin staff: administrative staff
*also the lecturer**: also the lecturers
it's not a bad number: it's quite a reasonable situation (colloquial)
*I have some relative was living**: I have some relatives who were living
*so I decide to come and join them**: so I decided to come and join them
*the first one I start**: the first one I started
made me redundant: Berry lost his job because there was no more work to do
*so I have to leave**: so I had to leave
Morris's/British Leyland: State owned British car manufacturing company
*which I get one**: which I got
*I work there**: I worked there
*I decide to stick it there**: I decided to stay there
*I have a luck with the girls**: I'm lucky with girls
*I decide to sell it for her**: I decided to sell it for her

Note

Berry's speech has been influenced by Caribbean English. An asterisk (*) against the appropriate Language item in the list indicates where this occurs.

Listening

1932 born
1960 left St Vincent
1971 left bakery
1980 left British Leyland
1985 is caretaker at college

B
1 T **2** F **3** F **4** N **5** F **6** F **7** T **8** N

C
3 ☑ **5** ☑

D
1 ☑ **5** ☑ **7** ☑ **8** ☑

Practice

A
1 What do you *actually* do?
2 So you work shifts, *do you*?
3 And when *did* you first *come* to England?
4 And how did you find *it, coming* to England?
5 (*And*) *why* did you come to Oxford?
6 So what did you do when you first *came* then?
7 *Did* you *have* a job to come to?
8 *Where was* your first job?
9 And why did you *leave* there?
10 You live just round the corner, *don't you*?
11 I hear that you sell cosmetics there too. *That's* rather unusual, *isn't it*?
12 *How* do you *actually* sell it to them?
13 So you *don't actually* do any demonstrations, or anything like that?
14 So how long *have you been* doing that then?
15 *So really*, you're helping her to sell?

B
1 What do you actually do?
Whereabouts in the West Indies?
2 When did you first come to England?
How did you find it, coming to England?
Why did you come to Oxford?
Where was your first job?
Why did you leave there?
3 So you work shifts, do you?
You live just round the corner, don't you?
4 So you don't actually do any demonstrations, or anything like that?

Speaking

Student A
Suitable questions might be:
Where were you born?
Your parents were Italian, weren't they?
Your father died when you were quite young, didn't he?
How did your mother finance your education?
You worked as a teacher while studying at night school. That must have been hard, mustn't it?
So what made you decide to enter politics?
So really, your weakness lies in your lack of experience in foreign affairs?

Student B
Suitable notes for the interview might be:
Women make up 53% of the voting population in the USA – it's about time a woman was given a key position in government to represent them. My background (immigrant parents, working mother, paying own night school fees) has given me insight into America's social problems which many of the country's politicians lack.
I feel that the way my career has developed, especially the varied experience I have gained since being elected Member of Congress for King's, will equip me very well for the job of President or Vice President.

10 Local government

This is part of a lecture, given in a lecture hall, to a large group of adult students at a further education college. The style is formal. Study the chart before listening for specific information.
Accent: RP

Tapescript

I'd like to talk about local government in England and Wales, and in England and Wales there are two main types of council. For instance, if I could take the example of Oxfordshire, there is one county council where they are responsible for education, social services, structure planning, highways, libraries and museums, and so on. And there are five district councils, again in Oxfordshire, and they're responsible for housing, council housing in particular, for local plans, for dustbin collection, environmental health, and they're also responsible for swimming baths, and in Oxford, for instance, they are building an ice-rink in the middle of the city.

If we could talk particularly about the question of education, I think this would illustrate the idea of local government in the best way possible. First of all, there is a minister at central government level. He is the Minister for Education and he's responsible for running a comprehensive education system in the whole country. But in practice there is a lot of local control. So local councils, county councils (Oxfordshire County Council is one example), actually run the schools and colleges in their area.

If we take the example of Oxfordshire again, there are seventy county councillors. They're elected every four years, mostly unpaid, except for their expenses, and about thirty of these are on the Education Committee, which meets regularly. And these councillors obviously make policy, but most of the work is done behind the scenes by the Chief Education Officer, who's a paid official, and his staff. And it's very much a question of the Chairman of the Education Committee, an elected councillor, running the service in conjunction with the Chief Education Officer (the official) and his staff.

If I could give an idea of some of the structure. There are three sub-committees: Education Committee itself, plus the Schools Committee, the Further Education Committee, and a General Services Committee.

One main issue which they're looking at at the moment, in fact all the time, is obviously the question of teachers. Pupil-teacher ratio, for instance. And that tells you how many teachers are employed by the council and how many children there are, giving you the number of children per class. And a lot of the opposition parties and parents and others are agitating all the time for smaller class sizes. For instance, in the primary schools, it's said by many people that to have classes of over thirty is unreasonable, and they should be reduced in size. It is of course expensive to employ teachers, so that's the argument on the other side.

Basically, the system, then, is a partnership between the Minister at central government level, who of course is a, an elected politician, by the staff in the Department of Education and Science, the civil servants, and by local councils, governors of schools, parents and teachers and so on. I suggest for discussion . . .

Language items

council: a group of people elected to advise on and organize the running of a local area
social services: State-provided welfare services
structure planning: (the local council's) strategy for building and development in the future
highways: roads
council housing: houses built and owned by the council and let to low-income families at a subsidized rent
dustbin collection: a service organized by the local council to collect and dispose of household rubbish
environmental health: condition of our surroundings, e.g. water, streets, air, etc.
councillor: an elected member of the council
issue: topic, subject for debate
opposition parties: the political parties which are not currently in power
agitate: to stir up concern or awareness
civil servant: person who works in the civil service, i.e. a government department
school governor: local person, often a councillor, who works voluntarily on a committee which helps in the policy-making of a school

Note

The money needed by a council for providing services comes partly from central government and partly from local taxes, known as 'rates'.

Listening

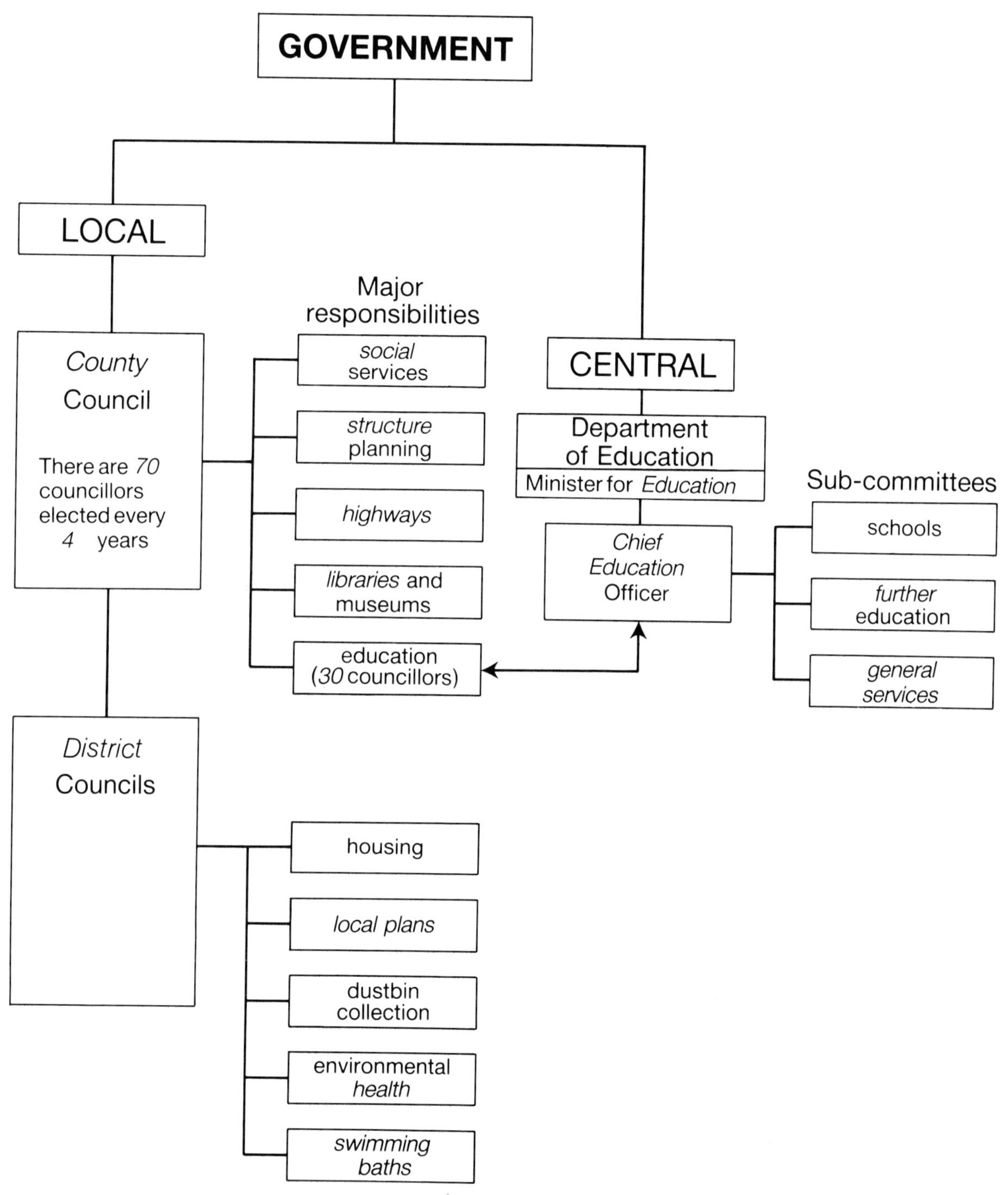

GOVERNMENT
LOCAL
CENTRAL
Major responsibilities
County Council
There are 70 councillors elected every 4 years
social services
structure planning
highways
libraries and museums
education (30 councillors)
Department of Education
Minister for Education
Chief Education Officer
Sub-committees
schools
further education
general services
District Councils
housing
local plans
dustbin collection
environmental health
swimming baths

Practice

A

1 If I *could take the example* of Oxfordshire.
2 . . . *for instance*, they are building an ice-rink in the middle of the city.
3 If we *could talk particularly* about the question of education.
4 . . . I think this *would illustrate* the idea of local government in the best way possible.
5 If we *take the example* of Oxfordshire again.
6 If I *could give an idea* of some of the structure.

Note

It would be inappropriate to use the above structures in conversation. They are used mainly in writing or in formal speech.

B

Some suitable ways of asking questions are suggested in the table below.

could you repeat		what you said about . . . ?
tell explain to	me	
		what you meant by . . . ?
would you mind repeating		
telling explaining to	me	what you said about . . . ?

11 Spot the sport

Each of the five extracts has a different style and accent. Students should listen for clues to identify the sport.
Accent: Australian; RP; London; Canadian; RP

Tapescript

1

Interviewer Well, congratulations, Don. You all did really well.

Don Yeah. Well, considering there was a very strong head w . . . head wind and we had the stream against us, we managed to rate quite well, I think.

Interviewer But there were some pretty close moments though, weren't there?

Don Yeah, there were a couple of them. That's when, er, I saw the other lot coming up behind us. It gave me quite a shock but er, we managed to pull away again. Course, it was a great help having such an experienced cox who er, knew the conditions.

Interviewer Well, thanks Don.

2

And finally, the second test. At the close of play today, England were 26 for no wickets, in reply to Pakistan's 449 for eight declared. And the time now is ten minutes past ten.

3

Colin I saw it on the telly. You – I mean, you were saying you go to matches and you don't see it. No hooliganism. I saw that match between England and France and, I mean, well, you didn't see much of the match 'cos of all the crowd behaviour. And I wa. . . I was ashamed, I was ashamed to be English.

Dave Oh no, mate, no.

Colin I mean they were waving Union J. . . and all, all, all that rubbish was coming from the English supporters.

Dave That was what the telly picked out. It wasn't like that at all.

Colin Well, what do you mean? It was happening. They just put the cameras on it. It was happening, ripping up seats and . . .

Dave It blows it up out of all proportion. It's not like that really. No, it isn't. I mean, honestly mate. I mean . . .

4

Interviewer Rita, how do you feel about meeting the top seed so early in the tournament?

Rita Er, well Mike, you know last year I, I drew the top seed in the first round, and, er, this year's just got to be better. I mean I've only played Georgina once and that was in a doubles, so this'll be different. Erm, and I've been watching her form this tournament and I think that if I can keep her away from the net, if I can keep her back, then I'll, I'll stand a good chance.

5

Only three clear rounds so far, and the fastest time ninety-five seconds. Una Patrick is very experienced on this sort of course. And there's the bell and . . . nice easy canter and . . . easily over the first jump. And oh! that is a tight turn. Is that too tight? She's coming up to the wall now . . . oh, and they're over. She, she's hit, she's hit a brick but it's stayed, oh! And another tight turn . . . and coming up to the last . . . oh dear! She's met that completely wrong. Oh-h dear, dear. Bad luck, Una. That's five faults. So we're left with still the clear, the three clear rounds.

Language items

cox: person who steers a (rowing) boat (abbreviation of *coxswain*)
test: one of the (cricket) matches in a tour played between two countries
England were 26: England had scored 26 runs
no wickets: no player was out
449 for eight declared: with a score of 449 and with eight players out, Pakistan decided to stop batting
telly: television (colloquial)
Union Jack: the British flag
It blows it up out of all proportion: it exaggerates unrealistically
mate: form of address used mainly by men (very colloquial)
top seed: (tennis) player graded number one
clear rounds: attempts (at show-jumping) which have been without fault or penalty
canter: speed between a trot and a gallop

Listening

A
1 e **2** f **3** b **4** e **5** a

B
1 h **2** j **3** k **4** n **5** p

Practice

The two tenses that are contrasted are the present continuous and the present perfect which are commonly used when giving an eye-witness account.

A
She*'s coming up to* the wall now – oh, and they*'re over*. She, she*'s hit*, she*'s hit* a brick but it*'s stayed*, oh! And another tight turn – and *coming up to* the last – oh dear! She*'s met* that completely wrong.

B
The two tenses that are contrasted are the simple past and the past continuous.
Examples of simple past: *I saw it on the telly, I saw that match, you didn't see much of the match, I was ashamed, that was what the telly picked out, it wasn't like that, they just put the cameras on it.*
Examples of past continuous: *you were saying, they were waving, it was happening.*

Note

The simple past tense denotes a definite, completed action. The past continuous is used to give background information and indicates an interest in the action itself as it is actually happening; its completion is not of interest. For example, *I was living in the USA when I met my future husband.*

12 Eccentrics

This is a light-hearted, informal conversation. Students should try not to be discouraged by the fast speed, but identify the features on the pictures and then listen for specific information.
Accent: RP; RP

Tapescript

Carole I like your brooch, Helen. That's new, isn't it?
Helen Yes, yes. You know that old lady who died – er, she was a recluse in Woodstock Road. Did you read about her?
Carole Oh yes, I did. I'd seen it . . . I'd, I'd also, of course, seen the house lots of times.
Helen Yes, well, I saw her once. Years ago you used to see her going up and down the Woodstock Road and I had a vivid memory of her. She used to ride a tricycle.
Carole A what?
Helen A tricycle.
Carole In those days that must have been extraordinary.
Helen Yes, and I saw her one day. Somebody pointed her out to me, and, and it was blazing sun and there she was in a sou'wester, and she had a sort of long flowing mackintosh and wellies. And she was singing at the top of her voice. And I, I always had this picture of her, and when I heard that she'd died, I went to the sale and I thought I just wanted to buy something.
Carole What sale?
Helen The sale of her effects. It'll be . . .
Carole Oh yes, that's right they had a . . . yes.
Helen Yes, it was an amazing house. It was three feet of filth. Incredible! The squatters had taken over, and she eventually had to land up er, living in the attic. It's a very sad story.

Carole So she lived in the same house as the squatters?

Helen Yeah. There were up to, sort of, 50 squatters at one time.

Carole It's interesting, most of the er, eccentrics one sees around the place are men. You don't see very many women, do you?

Helen Well, I don't know, I had a, an amazing uncle. He was the chaplain of a, in a . . .

Carole A what?

Helen . . . a chaplain in a psychiatric hospital. A priest. And he had a, a great friend. Somebody who, I think, fell in love with him, and she always used to dress as the Queen of Sheba. She had these fantastic flowing robes and feathers in her hair.

Carole All the time?

Helen Yes, all the time. And she expected him . . . everybody to bow and scrape when she came in, and as the years rolled, my uncle became more and more like the, the patients in the hospital. Erm, and I used to go and stay there when I was a child. And the wife, they had no children, she grew more and more like the dog. They were really an amazing couple. I really mourn their passing.

Carole Actually, I don't . . . I really don't know why I said that about women, because, in fact, of course there's that amazing woman in the British Museum Reading Room.

Helen Oh, tell me about her.

Carole You haven't heard about her? Oh, I thought she was entirely anecdotal but I did actually see her once. Erm . . . she . . . well, she was a perfectly ordinary-looking grey academic . . .

Helen Mm.

Carole . . . looked as though she spent her life in dusty university libraries, and she'd come in, she'd order up her books . . .

Helen Uhuh.

Carole . . . and she'd sit there for about ten minutes. And then suddenly, up she'd jump and she had one of these wrap-around skirts . . .

Helen Mm.

Carole . . . erm, and she'd unwrap it, whip it off and underneath were a pair of running shorts.

Helen I don't believe you . . .

Carole No, really, seriously. I didn't believe it the first time I saw it. Erm, and then she'd take out from her bag, not theses, but damn great boots, walking boots, but of course they had quite silent soles 'cos . . .

Helen Mm. Mm.

Carole . . . So, and then she'd just walk round and round and round.

Helen In the library?

Carole Yes, actually in the library. But not just casually walking. You know, that sort of moving-your-body-backwards-and-forwards sort of walking. She was amazing.

Helen The character that I had a great affection for is Mike. You know him.

Carole Mick, you mean.

Helen Oh, I . . .

Carole You call him Mike?

Helen I call him Mike. Anyway, you know the one I mean?

Carole Yeah.

Helen Because I see him, well I used to see him every day when I was cycling to and from work and he was always standing stationary, sort of whatever time of the day you went to, and then one day he wasn't there and I was really sad, and I thought he'd died. But he . . .

Carole They moved him, didn't they? Mm.

Helen They moved him and now he's near college, isn't he?

Carole Do you know, I saw him this morning.

Helen Did you?

Carole He's had a change of image. He was wearing a very smart sort of businessman's beige coat and a CND badge.

Helen Oh, that's lovely. Wouldn't it be sad if there weren't any eccentrics around?

Language items

eccentric: person who dresses and behaves unusually
recluse: person who lives alone and avoids other people
sou'wester: waterproof hat with a protective rim (see pictures 2 and 3)
wellies: waterproof rubber boots reaching to the knee (abbreviation of *Wellington boots*)
effects: goods, property (always plural)
land up: reach a final point
bow and scrape: show great respect for
anecdotal: not true, only existed in people's stories or anecdotes
theses: lengthy, written essays submitted for a university degree (singular: *thesis*)
C.N.D.: Campaign for Nuclear Disarmament

Listening

3 ☑ **5** ☑ **6** ☑ **8** ☑

Practice

A

1 I had *a vivid memory* of her.
2 I always *had this picture* of her.

B

1 I really *mourn their passing.*
2 The character *that I had a great affection for is Mike.*

C

The structure Carole uses is made with *would: she'd come in, she'd order up her books, she'd sit there for about ten minutes, up she'd jump, she'd unwrap it, she'd take out from her bag, she'd just walk round and round.*

Note

'Would' and 'used to' can both be used to express a past habit or action. 'Would' is typically used in narrative style when the speaker wants to emphasize the characteristic behaviour of someone. 'Used to' can also be used to talk about states and situations.

13 Dr Norton's surgery

The task requires listening for specific information. The practice material develops an awareness of the use of appropriate language to manipulate a situation.
Accent: Midlands; RP

Tapescript

Receptionist Warmington Health Centre. Can I help you?

Secretary Oh, good morning. I'd like to make an appointment for Mr Roger Pilkington today or tomorrow. He needs a cholera jab.

Receptionist Er, who's, er, Mr Pilkington's doctor?

Secretary Oh. It's Dr Norton.

Receptionist Dr Norton. Well, I'm afraid Dr Norton's not well himself. Erm, and we're very booked up today. In fact, er, we're back . . . booked up tomorrow as well.

Secretary Oh dear. Well, it is rather urgent because he's got to go to India on Friday unexpectedly. Erm, look, could he possibly see someone on Thursday?

Receptionist Well, Dr Wilder . . . now she's got two appointments available. There's one at 9.20 and there's one at 1.15.

Secretary Oh fine, I think the 9.20 appointment please.

Receptionist 9.20. Oh, he must bring his vaccination booklet. It's £2.80 that.

Secretary Yes. Yes, thank you. I'll remind him about that.

Receptionist Right.

Secretary Well, thank you very much indeed for your trouble. Goodbye.

Receptionist Goodbye.

Language items

health centre: local headquarters where medical services are available
jab: injection or vaccination (colloquial)
very booked up: very busy, have no more (appointments) available
vaccination: an injection of vaccine into a person to protect against disease

Listening

To: *Mr Pilkington*
Subject: *Doctor's appointment*
Arranged appontment re *cholera* vaccination for *Thursday* at *9.20* with Dr *Wilder* (Dr *Norton* ill).
Remember to take *vaccination booklet.*
Cost: *£2.80.*

Practice

1 I've got to have an appointment at once.
2 Dr Norton has a terrible hangover and told me to book in only real emergencies.
3 Can't you be more helpful?
4 It's essential.
5 He'll <u>have</u> to go on Thursday.
6 At last I'm getting somewhere!
7 Must hurry to catch Mr P. before he leaves.
8 Phew, that was lucky!

Speaking

Secretary I was wondering if I could have tomorrow off. I have a family problem that I'd like to sort out.

Boss Well, it's a bit difficult tomorrow. As you know, there's a lot of work on at the moment.

Secretary Would Friday be more convenient? It really *is* important.

Boss I suppose I *could* manage on Friday without you – I've a meeting in town all afternoon.

Secretary Well, that would be a great help. Thank you very much indeed.

Boss That's all right, but perhaps you could stay late one evening to catch up on the work.

14 After a fashion

The first costume museum guide has a competent, friendly approach and tries to entertain as well as instruct. The second has a far more formal, scholarly manner and his primary aim is to inform. Students should identify the features of the costumes in the pictures, then listen to match the pictures with the commentary.
Accent: RP; RP

Tapescript

Guide 1

Everybody over here, please. That's right – so you can see this display. Right. Now, here you can see what happened in the early eighteenth century. These are the sort of dresses that were worn at court, and they're obviously intended to demonstrate that the wearers were entirely ladies of leisure. Nobody, after all, could possibly attempt any sort of work with a skirt that was three metres wide. These skirts were kept in shape with a pannier, like two baskets underneath. And to manoeuvre yourself through doors you had to manipulate the panniers through slits in the side of the skirt . . . great emphasis was placed on materials and ornamentation. So, look at the beautiful embroidery. All hand done, of course. And the colours were made from natural dyes, flowers, berries, lichens, etc. Now, if you turn round and face the case opposite. Yes, that's right. Thanks. Well, here you can see a marked change by the middle of the century. The dresses had become less unwieldy, though in compensation the headdresses had become more so. The dresses now come in three parts, an underskirt, with an overdress which is more like a long coat, and a central part called a stomacher which links the other two parts. But, of course, the hair is the *pièce de résistance.* This became more and more elaborate as the century progressed. The hair was larded with goose grease and stretched over a frame and then powdered with flour, pounds of it. Uhuh. It was then ornamented with flowers, fruit, feathers, even a whole bird. The hairdressing was an incredibly complicated process, so it wasn't done very often. Women had to sleep sitting up in order not to disarrange it too much. It was probably only taken down and washed twice a year. So you can imagine how hair lice flourished. Now, if you'll pass on to the next room, my colleague will tell you about . . .

Guide 2

Ladies and gentlemen, could you please move a little closer so I don't need to shout – thank you. Now, the clothes you can see in this case were worn by women at the turn of the century. You'll notice a, a dramatic change from the fashions of the early 18th century, and most striking is the disappearance of the enormous wigs you saw earlier. The hair is now worn short and simple, er, the result of a tax on hair powder imposed by the government in 1795. The dresses are now a great deal simpler and more flowing, with high waists, and were much influenced by the French Empire line popular in France during the Napoleonic Wars, which followed the Revolution. The rich of both countries felt it unwise to flaunt their wealth any more, and their prosperity is subtly shown by the quality and quantity of the lace worn, very expensive and much prized. Dresses were frequently of white muslin and reflect the keen interest shown at that time in Ancient Greece.
Now, we'll move on to the Victorian case. Er, I'm sorry if I seem to be hurrying you, but do feel free to come back at the end and look more closely at the clothes. Now, we are in the year 1850. Queen Victoria was by then firmly established on the throne and she set an example of the 'ideal' woman who spent her time caring for her husband and family. Er, women's lives were restricted and the clothes of the period reflect this. Gone is the freedom of movement we saw in the Regency period. Once again, the wearer is constrained. First, a woman wore a 'cage' of whalebone, and over this were at least three frilled petticoats and on top a heavy full-length dress. What a weight to carry around! Now, no wonder Victorian ladies were not expected to participate in any sport, except formal dancing. As you see, there's much trimming of the dresses and the clothes were brightly coloured. This had only recently been made possible by the introduction of chemical dyes and the invention of domestic sewing machines. Er, come this way and we will move on . . .

Language items

court: royal palace
pannier: basket or supporting frame
dyes: substances for colouring material
lichens: small plants that grow on rocks or trees
unwieldy: awkward to move or control
stomacher: ornamental covering for the chest
pièce de résistance: most important or impressive item
larded: greased
lice: small, parasitic insects that live in human hair (singular: *louse*)

flaunt: to display in order to attract attention
muslin: thin, fine cotton material
Regency period: 1810-20 (in Britain)
whalebone: substance from the upper jaw of a whale used as stiffener

Listening

Picture 1; late 18th century
Picture 2; early 18th century
Picture 5; 1850
Picture 6; early 19th century

Practice

A
The items listed can be found in the following drawings.
overdress 1
underskirt 1
stomacher (covering for the chest) 1
headdress 1
frilled petticoat 5
frame (for hair) 1
cage (Victorian undergarment) 5
pannier (basket to keep wide skirt in shape) 2
embroidery 2; 3
lace 6
trimming 5
feathers 1
muslin 6

B
1 demonstrate manipulate participate

Note

'Elaborate' and 'complicated' are not used as verbs in this passage.

2 The suffix is -or.
manipulator demonstrator investigator commentator

3

deteriorate	commute	establish	distinguish
pollute	evacuate	tolerate	imitate
flourish	demolish	execute	refute
anticipate	dispute	implicate	diminish

15 At a loss for words

This is a casual but slightly academic conversation between friends. Students should listen for gist before listening intensively to complete the task.
Accent: French; RP

Tapescript

Alex Hello, Carole? Is that you?
Carole Alex! What on earth are you doing . . . a stupid question, you're doing the same as I am.
Alex What are you laughing at?
Carole Well, actually I'm just reading this article in *Punch*. It's the Franglais column. It's very funny.
Alex Oh, yes, yes, er . . .
Carole I know this is only a spoof, but I think these adaptions of English into French or French into English can be very funny. How does it occur actually?
Alex Oh, I suppose it came after the war, you know when the Americans were in France and a lot of English words and expressions came into French. Er . . .
Carole Oh, I see, yes, so . . .
Alex But after that there was a strong reaction against it, I think.
Carole You mean people don't . . . aren't very keen on it. A sort of linguistic imperialism.
Alex Exactly, yes, er, take the ex. . . example like 'lift' you see. We've got no, no word in French for lift.
Carole You mean lift, the thing that goes up and down . . .
Alex No, no. No, no, I mean, erm, would you like a lift home or something like that.
Carole Mm.
Alex Would you like a lift. What would you say in French? You would say something like, er, can I take you home with my car?
Carole Oh, I see, so . . .
Alex It's so much easier to say er, would you like a lift, you see.
Carole . . . I see so, in fact it's often for words that there is no equivalent for in . . .
Alex Yes, that . . . that's it, yes.
Carole . . . in French.
Alex Yes.
Carole Or something . . . I suppose the same would apply to something like erm, 'le weekend'.
Alex Yes, yes. That goes a bit . . . that goes back a bit. Yes, I suppose it was something er, before, even before the first World War.
Carole Oh, that one's really old. Are there any more recent examples?
Alex Er, oh yes. 'Speakerine' is a good example.
Carole Speakerine?

Alex Speakerine, yes.
Carole That doesn't even sound French. That sounds more German.
Alex Yes, it's a bit of a monster actually. You know, it means an announcer or a, a newsreader.
Carole Oh, I see, on the, on the box?
Alex Yes.
Carole And there are other things, aren't there, that are distortions like that. Erm . . . oh, what's the one I can, erm . . . 'le smoking' . . .
Alex Ah, le smoking, yes.
Carole . . . which means, er, dinner jacket in English . . .
Alex And we say smoking in French. It's very strange, in fact. But you've got another one, 'the training', the training. And you . . .
Carole What's that?
Alex Oh, it's like, it's like a pyjama in French. And you will say, I don't know, er . . .
Carole The pyjama?
Alex . . . children it's getting late, erm, put, put your training on and go to bed.
Carole How peculiar, because I mean, training means something quite different. Are there any other reasons why we borrow, why the French borrow words, borrow English words?
Alex Er, snob value, I suppose.
Carole Oh, really.
Alex Oh, yes. Er . . .
Carole You mean English words are snobbish in French?
Alex Yes. They would, they would take a word like 'building' and think it's much better to live in a building than to be – to live in a house.
Carole How strange, because building is such . . .
Alex So we say building; we are living in the building.
Carole It's such a mundane word in English. I mean, it sounds just so ordinary.
Alex Yes, it is.
Carole But surely, I mean something like 'le parking' which is very common, that, that can't have snob value, can it?
Alex No, no, of course, I mean just the French is cumbersome.
Carole Mm.
Receptionist Mrs Harding, could you go through now please.
Carole Oh dear! I've got to go.
Alex Bye, bye, Carole.
Carole I hope it's not too painful, Alex. Thanks, bye.

Language items

Punch: a humorous, monthly magazine
Franglais: corruptions of English words used in informal French
Franglais column: Punch has a regular feature on Franglais
spoof: parody
adaptions: adoptions (the speaker makes a slip)
the war: the Second World War, 1939–45
the box: television (colloquial)
a pyjama: pyjamas (always plural)
no, no, of course: no, no, of course not (the speaker is agreeing with a negative question)

Listening

A

Categories	Example 1	Example 2	Example 3
1 No equivalent word in French	*lift*	*weekend*	—
2 *distortions*	speakerine (means *announcer*)	*smoking* (means 'dinner jacket')	*training* (means 'pyjamas')
3 *snob value*	building	—	—
4 *French is cumbersome*	*parking*	—	—

B

1 c **2** b **3** a **4** c

Practice

A

1 People aren't very keen on it.
2 It's often for words that there's no equivalent for in French.
3 You mean English words are snobbish in French?
4 It sounds just so ordinary.

B

Verb	Related Noun	Related Noun A person or thing that . . .
think	a thought	a thinker (person)
1 laugh	1 *laughter* 2 *a laugh*	—
2 *express*	an expression	—

(*continued*)

(*continued from page 76*)

Verb	Related Noun	Related Noun A person or thing that . . .
3 *announce*	*an announcement*	an announcer (person)
4 *react*	a reaction	*a reactor* (thing)
5 occur	*an occurrence*	—
6 *imperialize*	imperialism	*an imperialist* (person)
7 *exemplify*	an example	—
8 *distort*	a distortion	*a distortionist* (person)
9 borrow	—	*a borrower* (person)
10 *build*	a building	*a builder* (person)

16 Waiting in the wings

This recording is apparently a radio interview with a famous actress. As the interview progresses, it becomes increasingly clear that the interviewer (who is young and inexperienced) is not in control. The interview is, in fact, a satire. It is typical, both in style and content, of the brief sketches broadcast on satirical radio and television shows. Students should be familiar with the theatrical terms listed under Language items, so that clues in the recording can be picked up as quickly as possible.
Accent: RP; RP

Tapescript

Interviewer Dame Kitty, it is with a mixture of pleasure and awe that I find myself here with you, in your dressing room at the Theatre Royal, Morecambe. Not only is it your eightieth birthday, but it is also your five hundredth performance in *The Rat Trap*. We're all hoping that you will give us a few intimate glimpses of your long and distinguished career. The play in which you made your name was Shaw's *Heartbreak House*, wasn't it?

Dame Kitty Yes, it was touring here at the time. I was only taken on as an understudy, of course, but I'd just spent three months in a musical version of *The Seagull*, so even then I . . .

Interviewer And then fate took a hand, and you took over the lead when the great Nelly Perry broke her leg.

Dame Kitty Fate? I pushed her! The old cow was too sozzled to notice.

Interviewer Erm . . .

Dame Kitty Mark you, she hung on pretty hard to the bannisters . . .

Interviewer Do, do tell us a, a little about how you came to take up a stage career. After all, coming as you did from a, a family of eleven children, living in the slums of Hackney, your father permanently drunk and out of work, it must have been a terrible struggle to get on.

Dame Kitty Wherever did you get all that rubbish?

Interviewer I beg your pardon?
Dame Kitty I suppose you've been reading my autobiography.
Interviewer Erm, well . . .
Dame Kitty All ghosted for me by some smart-alec at Grabbit and Grabbit, you know. 'Never sell a thousand copies,' he said to me, 'if you tell 'em your father was a respectable solicitor from Surbiton who . . .'
Interviewer Erm, quite, quite, quite . . . Erm, your first husband was, was a medical pioneer, I believe?
Dame Kitty Mm . . . Well, you could say that.
Interviewer Ah.
Dame Kitty He made a fortune out of *Dentribrite*, you know, the powdered stuff. You stick some in a mug of water, pop your false teeth in and it gets the muck off. Nellie Melba and I recorded a jingle for it. Now, now, now, how did it go . . . ?

Keep your teeth in Dentribrite
Overnight it turns 'em white . . .

Oh, that's right, do help yourself. Pour me another while you're at it.
Interviewer Er, er, coming back to your theatrical career, Dame Kitty . . .
Dame Kitty Uhuh.
Interviewer Erm, you approached the role of Juliet at, shall we say, a rather mature age, and the result wasn't one of your most memorable performances.
Dame Kitty Well, what do you expect? The director hardly ever took his eyes off Romeo, they were always rehearsing the bedroom scene without me . . .
Interviewer Ah, Shakespeare. Dame Kitty, erm, what part do you look back on with the most pleasure?
Dame Kitty Oh. That's easy. Arabella in *The Nun's Tragedy*.
Interviewer Really.
Dame Kitty Mm.
Interviewer What an unusual choice! You must have played all the great classical heroines. Erm, what was so special about Arabella?
Dame Kitty That moment in Act 5 when I managed to sink my teeth into that pompous old lecher Sir Lester Guthlaxton. You should have seen . . .
Interviewer Well, I, I think I just heard your five minute call, Dame Kitty. I can't thank you enough for allowing us to share some golden moments of your past. Many Happy Returns.
Dame Kitty Oh-h.
Interviewer Next week, *Waiting in the Wings* will be visiting the Grand Theatre, Blackpool . . .

Language items

wings: unseen area at the sides of a theatre stage
Dame: title awarded by the British government to women who have accomplished an outstanding achievement in their field
The Rat Trap: a fictional play title based on Agatha Christie's long-running murder play, *The Mouse Trap*
Shaw: George Bernard Shaw (1856–1950), British playwright and thinker
an understudy: an actor who studies the part of a principal actor in order to play that part if or when necessary
The Seagull: a tragic play by the Russian, Anton Chekhov; a musical version is highly unlikely
the lead: the principal part or role in a play
sozzled: drunk (colloquial)
mark you: conversational phrase used to draw attention to a point that contradicts a previous statement
bannisters: posts supporting the handrail of a staircase (the implication is that Dame Kitty pushed Nelly Perry down the stairs)
Hackney: inner-city district of London
ghosted: written by a professional writer (ghost), but in Dame Kitty's name
smart-alec: person who thinks himself/herself better than others and looks for opportunities to prove it (colloquial)
Grabbit and Grabbit: fictional name of Dame Kitty's publishers (the name suggests that they are money-grabbers)
Surbiton: a wealthy, respectable, commuter town in Surrey
jingle: advertising slogan set to music
Juliet } *Romeo* }: these references are to the heroine and hero of the play by Shakespeare (*Romeo and Juliet*) which tells the story of a teenage love affair and its tragic consequences
The Nun's Tragedy: a fictional Elizabethan play title
lecher: person inclined to excessive sexual thought, and/or associated activity
five minute call: back-stage announcement to actors to warn them that five minutes remain before their entry
Many Happy Returns (of the day): conventional birthday greeting wishing the recipient long life

Note

This recording is a satire on the rather reverent 'face to face' interview with a well-known personality common on British radio and television.

Listening

1 b **2** c **3** b **4** c **5** c **6** a **7** b **8** a **9** b **10** b

Practice

A

1 *And then* fate *took a hand*, and you took over the lead.
2 *Do tell us* a little *about* how you came to take up a stage career.
3 *Quite, quite, quite.* Your first husband was a medical pioneer, I believe?
4 *Coming back to your* theatrical career, Dame Kitty . . .
5 *Ah, Shakespeare.* Dame Kitty, what part do you look back on with most pleasure?
6 *Well, I think I just* heard your five minute call.

B

1 c **2** b **3** a **4** c **5** a **6** a

17 Jobspot

The fast delivery and informal style of this recording ('Hi', 'right', 'great', 'so there you go', etc.) are typical of a local radio station. Students should familiarize themselves with the chart before listening for specific information, much of which is repeated.
Accent: RP; West Country

Tapescript

David Hi! You're listening to Radio South West. The best in the south west for music and up-to-the-minute news. Sue's here. Hello, Sue.
Sue Hello, David.
David And we've got the Jobspot for you today. So, if you're unemployed or looking for a new job, this could be the spot for you. So, let's have a look, see what we've got today. How about a hairdresser? You must be experienced for this job and the pay will be agreed. So that will depend on experience. The hours are 8.30 to 5.00, Monday to Friday, and Saturday 8.45 to 1 p.m. So that's hours 8.30 to 5.00 Monday to Friday, and Saturday 8.45 to 1 p.m. A hairdresser. How about you, Sue, what have you got?
Sue Right, David. Well, the first one we've got is a cook. That's in a large, busy restaurant, so it's very useful to have had experience in large-scale cooking. The age is around twenty-five or so and the pay is £2 an hour. So that's not bad, is it? The hours are good too. That's Monday to Friday, 3.00 till 6.30.
David Great. Thanks, Sue. So that's a cook. Now, how do you fancy working out of doors? How do you fancy being a gardener? There's no age restrictions on this job. So as long as you're fit and strong, any age, that'll suit you. And if you're keen on gardening this could be a great job. The pay is £1.70 an hour. And the hours, Tuesday to Saturday, 8.30 to 5, Sunday you have to work once a month, but the bonus is that on Monday the Garden Centre's closed. Now, the sort of work you'd be doing is as a general assistant in the Garden Centre, potting, watering, things like that. So, if you've got green fingers, how about applying for that? Pay, £1.70 an hour. Sue, what else have you got?
Sue Right, Dave. Well, from outdoors to indoors. We've got a shorthand typist job here – that's in an office. And this job might suit a woman with school-age children, because the hours are only fifteen hours a week. The age is twenty to forty-ish and the pay depends on that age. It's a small, friendly office, but there is experience of course, but accuracy is more important than the experience. So, there you go. That's a nice shorthand typist's job in an office.
David Great. Here's a job possibly for somebody who's a school-leaver. It's, er, requires no experience at all, but training will be given on the job. And the pay is £67 a week. What's the job? Well, it's a shop assistant in a busy supermarket. It's a full-time job, but the big thing is, you don't need any experience. So, if you're just leaving school and fancy working in a supermarket, try that. You get one day off during the week and you must work one late evening till 9.30 p.m. OK? So that's a shop assistant. Well, if you fancy any of those jobs, give us a ring here on Jobspot at Radio South West. And now back to the music.

Language items

there's no age restrictions: there are no age restrictions
potting: placing plants in a flower pot
green fingers: skill in gardening
on the job: while working

Listening

A

Job	Full-time	Part-time	Experience essential	Experience useful	Experience not necessary	Age	Pay	Hours
hairdresser	√		✓			*N*	*to be agreed*	Monday–Friday *8.30–5.00* Saturday *8.45–1.00*
cook		✓		✓		*about 25*	£2 per hour	*Monday–Friday 3.00–6.30*
gardener	✓			*N*		*any*	*£1.70* per hour	Monday *off* Tuesday–Saturday *8.30–5.00* Sunday *once a month*
shorthand typist		✓		✓		*about 20–40*	*depends on age*	*15 hours a week*
shop assistant	✓				√	*suit school-leaver*	*£67* per week	*6 days a week one late evening a week (9.30 p.m.)*

B

1 watering, potting **2** fitness, strength

Practice

A

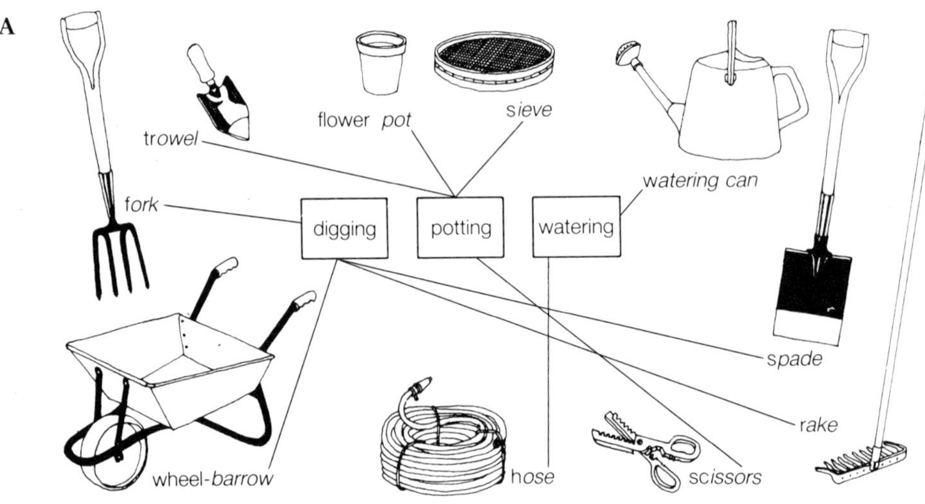

B

Electrician: plug, flex, screwdriver, fuse
Doctor: stethoscope, thermometer, syringe, bandage
Garage mechanic: jack, spanner, wrench, gauge
Carpenter: chisel, plane, saw, hammer

C

1 be keen on ('And if you're keen on gardening . . .')
2 How about -ing?
How do you fancy -ing?

Note

'How about . . .?' and 'How do you fancy . . .?' can be constructed with either a verb ending in '-ing' (*How do you fancy being a gardener?*), or a noun (*How about a hairdresser?*).

18 Help!

This recording consists of one side of a phone conversation. The point of the exercise is for listeners to pick up the clues and work out what the caller is asking Liza to do. It is not important to get the right answer – this exercise is meant to be fun! A recording of the full conversation follows the one-sided version for comparison after Practice.
Accent: American (southern); American

Tapescript

Hello . . . Oh sure. Well, I'd be glad to help out. Just anything you want . . . Oh, how wonderful! Oh, I wish I could get away on holiday . . . Oh! Er, well, the only thing is, how many of them are there? . . . Oh well, that's okay then . . . Well, let me think. Er, well, we did have one. Yeah, I think we still got it. But you know, it's pretty worn out and a bit dirty, not too nice, you know . . . Oh no! Why, I'm a little nervous about it now. I mean, er, I mean, I don't know if I can cope with that . . . Eight? Why, that, that's just a little too many. I mean, oh I, I don't think I could cope with that, I mean. And, and how do I tell when they're due, you know, when, when they're going to be there? . . . Well, what kind of food do I have to give them? . . . Well, does it have to be hot? I mean, why do you keep them? I mean, don't they cause you an awful lot of work and trouble? . . . Well, here's an idea. Why don't you bring what they need, then I'll just have – then I won't have to worry about it . . . Well, how fresh do they have to be? I mean, carrots keep a long time, specially in the cellar . . . A sack? How long did you say you were going to be away? . . . Well, I sincerely hope not, I mean, I'm not used to this sort of thing, you know . . . Okay, well yeah. You, you can help me get it all ready and organized and – 'cos I'm a little nervous about it, you know . . . Bye bye then.

Liza Hello.
Friend Hi, Liza. Look I'm sorry to bother you so late. I just wanted to ask you a little favour.
Liza Oh sure. Well I'd be glad to help out. Just anything you want.
Friend Look, sweetheart. I'm, erm, I'm going up to New York for a week.
Liza Oh, how wonderful! Oh I wish I could get away on holiday.
Friend Look, I got a problem though. I – you know I got some pet rabbits and er I, I, I need a home for them.
Liza Oh! Er, well, the only thing is, how many of them are there?
Friend Well, there's only two.
Liza Oh well, that's okay then.
Friend Oh thanks. That's absolutely terrific. Look, there's a tiny little problem though. Erm, I can't get their hutch out of my back yard. Would you happen to have one?
Liza Well, let me think. Er, well, we did have one. Yeah, I think we still got it. But you know it's pretty worn out and a bit dirty, not too nice, you know.
Friend Well, erm, I think that'll be all right. I, I'm sure it'll be fine just as long as you clean it up. I mean, you will have to clean it up because er, er, well, I didn't, didn't want to mention this earlier perhaps, but er, one of them's pregnant, you see. One of the rabbits is pregnant and she's going to be delivering er, her litter pretty soon.
Liza Oh no! Why, I'm a little nervous about it now. I mean, er, I mean, I don't know if I can cope with that.
Friend Course you can! Look, I mean, they're okay. She looks after her babies. She had eight last time. You'll love them.
Liza Eight? Why, that's just a little too many. I mean, oh I, I don't think I could cope with that, I mean. And, and how do I tell when they're due, you know, when, when they're going to be there?
Friend Very simple. You see the mother go off in the corner and she'll collect up a lot of her old fur and she'll start to make a little nest in the corner. And then when she does that, you'll know that she's ready to have the babies.
Liza Well, what kind of food do I have to give them?
Friend Very simple. Just bread and milk
Liza Well, does it have to be hot? I mean, why do you keep them? I mean, don't they cause you an awful lot of work and trouble?
Friend Oh honey, they're so sweet. They're so beautiful. You're going to just love them when you see them. They're so nice. Er, look , they also need a lot of fresh vegetables.
Liza Well, here's an idea. Why don't you bring what they need, then I'll just have – then I won't have to worry about it.
Friend Well, I, I could do that. But look, the vegetables have to be very, very fresh.
Liza Well, how fresh do they have to be? I mean carrots keep a long time, specially in the cellar.
Friend Okay, okay. I, I'll bring the sack of carrots then. That, that should be okay.
Liza A sack? How long did you say you were going to be away?
Friend Now look, honey. Don't start worrying too much. She may not produce these little bunnykins this week at all.
Liza Well, I sincerely hope not. I mean, I'm not used to this sort of thing, you know.

Friend You just sit tight. I'll come around in a couple of hours and we'll get your hutch all cleaned out and ready, okay?
Liza Okay, well, yeah. You, you can help me get it all ready and organized and – 'cos I'm a little nervous about it, you know.
Friend Okay. I'll see you later, sweetie.
Liza Bye bye, then.

Language items

sure: of course (American English)
I didn't want to mention this earlier: I should have mentioned this earlier (the speaker makes a slip)
due: the date or time when something is expected

Listening

1 b **2** a **3** b **4** b **5** a **6** a **7** a **8** b **9** a

Practice

A
1 *Well, the only thing is,* how many of them are there?
2 Oh no! Why, I'm *a little nervous about it* now.
3 Why, that's just a little too many. I mean, oh I don't *think I could cope with that.*
4 Well, I sincerely hope not. I mean, I'm *not used to this sort of* thing.

B
1 I mean
2 You know

Speaking

The following kind of phrases could be used.

Student A
I've got a favour to ask you . . .
I wonder if you could . . .
Would you mind . . .
Do you think you could possibly . . .
There's just one small thing . . .

Student B
Yes, of course . . .
I'd be happy to help . . .
Well, I'm not sure if I could manage that . . .
Well, I suppose it would be all right if you brought round the cat food . . .
I don't know if I'll have time to mow the lawn as well . . .
Couldn't you ask your neighbour to water the plants . . .?

19 Coping

In the early part of this conversation between two women, Teresa is tentative in her questioning. Her role is to show genuine interest and to prompt Pauline so as to encourage her to go on talking.
Accent: RP; RP

Tapescript

Teresa Is that a photo of your children?
Pauline Oh, yes. That's, that's Anna. Er, she's trying to be an opera singer.
Teresa Really.
Pauline My son's married. He's an engineer. That's Mike and er, Andrew's the youngest. He's nineteen. He's mentally handicapped.
Teresa Oh. I, I'm sorry. I had no idea.
Pauline Oh, no, please. That's quite all right. Er, I, I don't mind talking about him a bit.
Teresa Erm, did you know right from the beginning when he was born?
Pauline Well, he was very, very ill as a baby. Erm, so we knew that something was seriously wrong but we didn't know what it was at first. It's known most often as mongolism but it's Down's syndrome.
Teresa Ah, yes.
Pauline You can tell by looking at him and that's really quite useful because it means that people sort of have some understanding that there's something wrong.
Teresa Mm, mm.
Pauline They don't, you know, they don't expect too much and . . . well obviously his intelligence is very low. Erm, speech is one of the biggest problems. Er, he does have a lot of difficulty in communicating.
Teresa Mm. That must be very frustrating for him.
Pauline Oh, I think it's probably about the most frustrating thing, you know, he's got.
Teresa Mm.
Pauline Most things he, he, er, copes very well – socially for example. Erm, we can take him anywhere really.
Teresa Mm. What does he enjoy doing?
Pauline Oh, well. He can do quite a lot of things. He helps in the house a certain amount.
Teresa Uhuh.
Pauline He, er, he works in the garden. He really, he likes to help people and . . .

Teresa Mm.
Pauline . . . you know. And he loves to oh, play snooker, for example. Actually he can ride. He can ride a horse. Erm . . .
Teresa Oh really!
Pauline Erm, he swims really quite well.
Teresa Erm, and how, how well can he look after himself?
Pauline Oh. Well, not at all really. He's never going to be able to be independent. Erm, when I say not at all, I mean he, he'll put two pairs of socks on instead of one and he'll forget to put a coat on in winter, things like that. But, on the other hand, he, you know, he can wash and dress and things like that in a reasonable sort of way.
Teresa And can he get about on his own? Can he . . .
Pauline Oh, well. Er, that does have a bit, a few problems. You see, I mean, he wouldn't be able to ask his way if he got lost.
Teresa Mm.
Pauline Erm, he might get on a bus and nobody would quite know where he was going.
Teresa Ah, that's difficult.
Pauline Oh, he doesn't understand money either. Erm, I suppose our biggest worry is the fact that, er, you know, he might meet up with a group of yobos . . .
Teresa Mm.
Pauline . . . who'd be, be vicious or unkind to him.
Teresa Yes.
Pauline Actually, that did happen once and it's, er, you know, it's very difficult to forget about it.
Teresa How, how do you feel about his future?
Pauline Well, one never really stops having anxieties, but that's not (there) all, that's not all there is to it. He, he has a sort of, a sort of gift for happiness and he, he continually learns new skills, which is, is very exciting for him and it's, it's really lovely for us too. Erm . . .
Teresa I do hope I can meet him one day.
Pauline . . . well, everybody's much more understanding about things nowadays . . .
Teresa Mm.
Pauline . . . and people do find him nice.
Teresa Mm.
Pauline We're not the only ones who do.
Teresa Mm.

Language notes

Down's syndrome: a chromosome defect resulting in mental retardation
snooker: game played with twenty-one balls on a billiard table
yobos: hooligans

Listening

A
1 c **2** b **3** b **4** a

B
1 F **2** T **3** T **4** F

Practice

A

1 handicapped
2 had no idea
3 a bit
4 at first
5 low
6 communicating
7 frustrating
8 copes
9 enjoy
10 a certain amount
11 for example
12 look after
13 instead of
14 but, on the other hand
15 on his own
16 his way
17 quite know
18 anxieties
19 gift
20 nowadays

B
1 Really. **2** Oh. **3** Ah, yes. **4** Mm. **5** Uhuh.

20 And later today

This recording is typical of BBC Radio 4, a station catering for people with average educational backgrounds and tastes. Here, the broadcaster is giving a swift round-up of forthcoming programmes, with short extracts of some, in order to encourage listeners to switch on later in the day. The language, though scripted, is written to be spoken and is meant to sound spontaneous. Note that not all the mistakes in the text are marked. Students should predict alternatives where words are queried, and then listen to check predictions, before listening again for unmarked errors.
Accent: RP; RP; RP

Tapescript

Broadcaster . . . studio production was by Brendan Donavan and the editors were Francis Barnes and Derek Newton. And before the nine o'clock news, a quick look at some of this morning's highlights. At five past nine, there's *Science Tomorrow* with Jean Hook, and that's followed by *The World Around Us*, when we learn all about antipodean curiosities, how the platypus won his spurs and why baby kangaroos are called joeys. That's *Babies of the Bush*, at nine thirty. After *Tale at Ten*, the first in a new series of theatrical profiles, under the title, *Waiting in* *the Wings*. And this morning, Ray Keeling talks to the grand old theatrical dame, Kitty Spurge.

Interviewer The play in which you made your name was Shaw's *Heartbreak House*, wasn't it?
Dame Kitty Yes, it was touring here at the time. I was only taken on as an understudy, of course, but I'd just spent three months in a musical version of *The Seagull*, so even then I . . .
Interviewer And then fate took a hand, and you took over the lead when the great Nelly Perry broke her leg.
Dame Kitty Fate? I pushed her!

Broadcaster For more of Dame Kitty's colourful reminiscences, tune in at ten fifteen for *Waiting in the Wings*. Later, at two minutes past eleven, an examination of socialist agricultural policies worldwide when the Spectrum team presents *Let Them Eat Cake*. Finally, at eleven forty-five, today's concert, when the Bognor Philharmonic, under the baton of Wanda van Ek, will be bringing us Elgar's Sea Songs sung by Evadne Butcher.

Language items

antipodean: from the opposite sides of the earth, especially Australasia
platypus: Australian mammal with duck-like beak and flat tail
the bush: wild, uncultivated land of Australia
Dame: title awarded by the British government to great women who have accomplished an outstanding achievement in their field
let them eat cake: a remark attributed to Queen Marie-Antionette of France (late eighteenth century) when told that her subjects had not enough bread, and thought to typify the ignorant and indifferent attitude of the upper classes to the poor

Listening

The transcription below shows the typist's errors. Shaded areas indicate the mistakes already marked in the student's text.

```
Studio production was by Brendan Donavan, and the editors were
Francis Barnes and (Eric) Newton. ^ Before the nine o'clock news, a
quick look at (one) of this morning's (headlines.) At five (to) nine
(theirs) Si?gns Tomorrow with Jean Hook, and (it's) followed by
The (Wall) Around Us, when we learn ^ about antipodean curiosities,
how the platypus (wore) his (spure) and why ^ kangaroos are called
joeys.  Tha(t i)s Babies of the (Pouch) at nine thirty.  After Tale
at Ten, the first in a new ^ of theatrical profiles, (with) the
title Waiting in the Wi?nd.  And this morning Ray Keeling talks
to the ^ old theatrical dame, Kitty Spurge.
(Excerpt)
Fo?rmer of Dame Kitty's colourful reminiscences, (turn on) at ten
(fifty) for Waiting in the (Wind.) Later at two minutes past
eleven, an examination of (socialistic) agricultural (policis)
world ^ when the Spectrum ^ presents Let them eat (Coke.)
Finally, at eleven forty ^ (nine,) (today is a) concert, when the
Bognor Philharmonic, ^ the baton of Wanda van Ek will be
bringing us Elgar ^ Sea Songs sung by Evadne Butcher.
```

Practice

A

production title editors profiles studio series presents highlights tune in team

B

production — direction
portraits — profiles
editors — scriptwriters
serial — series
studio — set
features — highlights
presents — introduces
switch on — tune in
credits — title
group — team

C

editors — *to edit*
highlights — *to highlight*
serial — *to serialize*
portrait — *to portray*
team — *to team up with*
production — *to produce*

Speaking

For the purposes of accuracy, only the accented syllable of the stressed words has been underlined.

Tower Bridge is closed until early on Monday morning, so use London Bridge or Blackwall Tunnel. In Kent, Maidstone town centre's closed because of a carnival. Avoid that if you're driving. As you've heard, there's been motor racing at Brand's Hatch today, so expect very heavy traffic on the A20 between Dartford and Wrotham as the crowds leave. If you are going tomorrow and you want to join the M25 from the M1, leave the M1 at junction 7, the St Alban's exit, take the M10, then the A405, and the A6 to the M25 which you can join at South Mimms at junction 23.

Language items

Brand's Hatch: a motor-racing circuit in Kent
A20: an 'A' road is a major road
M25: an 'M' road is a motorway
junction: a motorway exit

The passage is a traffic announcement taken from a radio news programme. The information comes from a variety of sources including the Department of Transport and the Automobile Association, while some commercial radio stations have their own helicopters flying above major cities and reporting direct on traffic conditions.

21 Fairground Dream

This is a pop song with two familiar themes: love at first sight and unrequited love. The setting is a fairground. Students should first listen for gist, then read the lyrics to predict the missing words, before listening intensively to complete the task. Accent: RP

Tapescript

Fairground Dream

The fair was in town for a couple of days
One midsummer *evening* with the sky *ablaze*
I *strolled* among the sideshows
When *crash!* I saw this vision.

Tall and smiling with an easy *air*
The sunlight *glinted* on his long blond hair
I felt a *strange* emotion
I had to *move* in closer.

There was *nobody* with him
That I *could* see
But when I came *right* up to him
I *couldn't* speak.

I *followed* him the whole fair through
The caterpillar and the dodgems *too*
Once close *enough* to touch him
I didn't have the *courage*.

The *later* it got, the less it felt real
I followed him onto the Ferris *wheel*
We *cleared* the trees together
In separate *cars* again, though.

I saw his car stop *below* me
He rejoined the *crowd*
But when I got out of my car
He was *nowhere* to be found.

I didn't stop *looking* till I knew he'd gone
The wheel was black against the setting *sun*
He'd gone, he'd gone for *ever*
My fairground *dream* was over.

Language items

caterpillar: a vehicle that moves up and down like a caterpillar (an insect) on a circular track
dodgems: small electrical cars which take two passengers and are driven around a large circular floor; the aim is to dodge (avoid hitting) all the other cars
Ferris wheel: a huge wheel which rotates passengers in small cars

Note

The language items above are all typical attractions at any fairground in Britain.

Listening

The answers to this exercise are those words printed in italics in the tapescript on page 85.

Practice

A

days — ablaze   air — hair
wheel — real   too — through

B

see — pea, key /si:/ /pi:/ /ki:/
speak — week, antique /spi:k/ /wi:k/ /æntì:k/
crowd — loud, vowed / kraʊd / /laʊd/ /vaʊd/
found — sound, drowned / faʊnd/ /saʊnd/ /draʊnd/
gone — shone, swan /gɒn/ /ʃɒn/ /swɒn/
sun — fun, none /sʌn/ /fʌn/ /nʌn/

22 What's on?

This recording is of a conversation between two close friends. Students will be exposed to colloquial language spoken at fast conversational speed. The purpose of the task is selective listening focussed on Lizzie's plans; total comprehension is not necessary for its completion.
Accent: RP; RP

Tapescript

Ben Do you want another drink, Lizzie?
Lizzie Er, no thanks, I'll finish this.
Ben I'll tell you what, we've got to decide what we're going to do tomorrow.
Lizzie Well, what time do you want to meet?
Ben Oh, not too early. Look, let, let's meet in the morning. About eleven.
Lizzie Yeah, OK then. What about that exhibition, Colin Baxter?
Ben Oh, yeah. I, I read about that. What the photos . . .
Lizzie Yeah, that's right. Landscape photos. That should be good.
Ben OK. See you there at eleven. Look . . .
Lizzie OK then.
Ben Look, what else are we going to do?
Lizzie Oh, do you know what? I met those people. I met some of the cast in erm, *New Zone West.*
Ben Oh yeah.
Lizzie They could get us in free if you want to go to that.
Ben Free?
Lizzie Yeah.
Ben Oh yes, yeah. Let's go to that.
Lizzie OK then. We'll do that. Then what?
Ben Look, look I'll take you to the Assembly Rooms. You haven't been, have you?
Lizzie Yeah, we could go there for lunch.
Ben Yeah, they've got a really nice bar with, with food and things.
Lizzie Oh yes, and there's the mime thing on at the Assembly Rooms after that.
Ben Oh no, not mime!
Lizzie Oh, go on.
Ben No, I really don't like mime. I don't want to go.
Lizzie Oh, Ben. I really wanted to go to that.
Ben No, come to this South African thing. It's called, it's called *The Hungry Earth.* I read about it yesterday.
Lizzie But, but it's David Glass's last performance.
Ben Ah, look, anyway, you said you wanted to go to *The Tempest.* That starts at 3.35 . . .
Lizzie Yeah.
Ben . . . and David Glass doesn't finish until 3.35, so you can't go to both.
Lizzie Oh, all right. OK, so *The Hungry Earth* then.
Ben Yeah.
Lizzie What's that?
Ben I don't know. It's been really well reviewed. South Africa . . .
Lizzie Oh, political propaganda, huh?
Ben No, not at all. Not at all.
Lizzie OK then.
Ben Anyway, so, so after that, it's the Shakespeare.
Lizzie OK then. I think we're going to need some light relief after that, actually.
Ben What's that . . .
Lizzie How about *Accidental Death of an Anarchist.*
Ben Well, I tell you what, before, before we go out in the evening, I've got to go and meet some people at The Circuit and have, have some supper.
Lizzie Oh, OK then. I'll go back and meet, visit my relatives.
Ben Oh, right.
Lizzie Better fit that in some time, I suppose.
Ben But I've seen *Accidental Death* on the telly.
Lizzie Oh go on, it's supposed to be really funny and we're going to need some light relief after *The Tempest.*
Ben No, there's this dance performance on.

Lizzie Oh Ben! You, you've told me *Accidental Death*'s good, you're always telling me to go and see it.
Ben No, I know. You must go and see it.
Lizzie All right, oh OK, we'll split up.
Ben Look, I'll go to the dance and you go to that.
Lizzie OK then. And where do you want to meet, after that?
Ben Let's go to the revue. You know, the *Newsrevue.*
Lizzie Oh that's supposed to be satirical, isn't it?
Ben Well, I hope so.
Lizzie OK then. We'll do that. And then what?
Ben Oh no. What we must go to is Urgent Theatre . . .
Lizzie Oh, just . . .
Ben *Heartbreakers.*
Lizzie . . . 'cos you've got friends in the cast.
Ben No, no, no. Not at all, but it's brilliant. It's absolutely brilliant, so I'm told.
Lizzie OK then. All right, we'll go to that. Oh, and you know what? Tom Robinson's playing as well.
Ben Oh, look, look, we've got, we've got, we're going to about nine things already tomorrow, Lizzie.
Lizzie That's true.
Ben We're going to be so broke.
Lizzie That's going to be really expensive, isn't it?
Ben It's hopeless.
Lizzie Good grief. Oh, do you know what? I've been invited to a party. We could go to that instead if you want.
Ben Oh yeah. Whose is that?
Lizzie It's erm, Dave Scott's.
Ben Oh what, Dave Scott we met the other day? Oh no . . .
Lizzie Yeah. *The* Dave Scott.
Ben Yeah.
Lizzie OK. We'll do that then. Save a bit of money, I suppose.
Ben Right then.

Language items

I'll tell you what: / *do you know what?:* informal phrase used in conversation to introduce a new idea or suggestion
some light relief: something which is not serious or demanding
telly: television (colloquial)
be broke: have no money (slang)

Listening

Photographic exhibition (by Colin Baxter)
New Zone West
The Hungry Earth
The Tempest
Accidental Death of an Anarchist
Newsrevue
Heartbreakers

Practice

A
1 *Let's meet* in the morning.
2 *What about* that exhibition?
3 We *could go* there for lunch.

B
1 *OK.* See you there at eleven.
2 *We'll* do that.
3 *We'll* go to that.

C
1 Oh *no, not* mime!
2 I *really don't like* mime.

Speaking

Language items

squash: game played in a walled court with raquets and a rubber ball
tartan: Scottish woollen fabric woven with coloured stripes
ramble: country walk
loch: lake (Scottish)

23 A Hollywood story

The style of the anecdote is informal, and the speed fast. It is an unscripted, unprepared story, although it is told with unusual fluency. This suggests that it is a story the actor has told a number of times before. Students should first listen for gist, then use the clues in the questions and recording to complete the task.
Accent: American

Tapescript

A friend of mine who came from Australia, er, went to Hollywood. And in fact he'd only been there a few weeks when he got a call from his agent. And his agent said, 'Brucie, baby. Great news, fellow. They want you on the set of *Pillow Talk* tomorrow morning.' Now *Pillow Talk*, as you may or may not remember, was a, was a film with Rock Hudson and Doris Day, which was made in the sixties. Rock Hudson was a very big star then, so was Doris Day. Thing was, the studios were going broke at that time, and to try to get extra sources of money what they started doing was having coach tours of the studios. They'd bring in lots of tourists who would go through the studio sets and what they really wanted – the highlight of this tour – was always going to be to find and spot a star. Er, so they were allowed to go into areas where the actors actually took their recreation, their, their leisure – in the canteen, and then the er, rest areas, things like that. What the tourists didn't know was that the moment they approached there was always a look-out who would say, 'They're coming everybody, make for cover, they're all coming,' and all the actors, all the stars, would go away quickly, so the tourists didn't see anybody.

My friend, being new to the situation, didn't know what he was supposed to do, or what to expect, and he was sitting in the canteen quietly having his lunch on his first day, when somebody burst in through the doors and said, 'They're coming everybody, out, get out, everybody out,' and everybody went. He sat there in a confused state, with a couple of other people who were wearing overalls and had paint on them and were obviously working on the set, and he didn't quite know what to do. In came this whole load of people, with sun glasses and rhinestones on them, and blue rinsed hair, looking panicly around for somebody to corner, and one lady rushed up to him and said, 'Excuse me, excuse me, but are you anybody?'

Language items

baby: friendly form of address (American colloquial)
blue rinsed hair: (white or grey) hair that has been coloured with a blue rinse
leisure: /liːʒər/(American) /leʒə/ (British)
panicly: in panic
rhinestones on them: imitation diamonds on the sun glasses (Blain's description is of a middle-aged, American female stereotype)

Listening

A
1 e **2** c **3** a **4** j **5** o **6** g **7** b
8 m **9** i **10** k **11** d **12** n **13** f **14** l **15** h

B
1 T **2** T **3** F **4** F **5** T **6** F **7** F **8** T

Practice

A
1 a **2** a **3** a **4** b **5** c **6** c **7** c **8** c

B
1 a) Now b) Thing was
2 as you may or may not remember

C
They'*d* bring in lots of tourists who *would* go through the studio sets.
There was a look-out who *would* say . . .
All the stars *would* go away quickly.